D1563305

Taxation, Incomplete Markets, and Social Security

Munich Lectures in Economics
Edited by Hans-Werner Sinn

The Making of Economic Policy: A Transaction Cost Politics Perspective, by Avinash Dixit (1996)

The Economic Consequences of Rolling Back the Welfare State, by A. B. Atkinson (1999)

Competition in Telecommunications, by Jean-Jacques Laffont and Jean Tirole (2000)

In cooperation with the council of the Center for Economic Studies of the University of Munich

Martin Beckman, David F. Bradford, Gebhard Flaig, Otto Gandenberger, Franz Gehrels, Martin Hellwig, Bernd Huber, Mervyn King, John Komlos, Richard Musgrave, Ray Rees, Bernd Rudolph, Agnar Sandmo, Karlhans Sauernheimer, Klaus Schmidt, Hans Schneeweiss, Robert Solow, Joseph E. Stiglitz, Wolfgang Wiegard, Charles Wyplosz

Taxation, Incomplete Markets, and Social Security

The 2000 Munich Lectures

Peter A. Diamond

The MIT Press
Cambridge, Massachusetts
London, England

© 2003 Massachusetts Institute of Technology

All rights reserved. No part of this book may be reproduced in any form by any electronic or mechanical means (including photocopying, recording, or information storage and retrieval) without permission in writing from the publisher.

This book was set in Palatino on 3B2 by Asco Typesetters, Hong Kong. Printed and bound in the United States of America.

Library of Congress Cataloging-in-Publication Data

Diamond, Peter A.
  Taxation, incomplete markets, and social security : the 2000 Munich lectures / Peter A. Diamond.
    p.   cm. — (Munich lectures in economics)
  Includes bibliographical references and index.
  ISBN 0-262-04213-4 (alk. paper)
  1. Welfare economics. 2. Welfare state. 3. Taxation. 4. Capitalism.
5. Social security—Finance. 6. Taxation—Germany. 7. Capitalism—
Germany. 8. Social security—Germany—Finance. I. Title. II. Series.
HB846 .D53 2003
330.12′6—dc21   2002071769

For Kate, Matt, and Andy, with even more love.

Contents

Series Foreword

Every year the CES council awards a prize to an internationally renowned and innovative economist for outstanding contributions to economic research. The scholar is honored with the title "Distinguished CES Fellow" and is invited to give the "Munich Lectures in Economics."

The lectures are held at the Center for Economic Studies of the University of Munich. They introduce areas of recent or potential interest to a wide audience in a nontechnical way and combine theoretical depth with policy relevance.

Hans-Werner Sinn
Professor of Economics and Public Finance
Director of CES
University of Munich

Laudation for Peter A. Diamond

Many years ago, in fact in the summer of 1962, I first visited MIT; but I missed Peter, which was a shame. He was spending the summer at RAND, an American government research center, where they studied military strategy, game theory, and all that. He already had a high reputation at MIT, although he had arrived there only in 1960 to do an economics Ph.D. That followed a mathematics degree with highest honors at Yale, completed at the early age of twenty. Certainly his game-theory interlude, if one could call it that, did not hold him back, though game theory had little part in his publication over the years.

Rumor has it that early in 1963 he asked Bob Solow, one of his supervisors, how he was doing on the two papers he had already written. When Bob told him that he needed another one to complete his thesis, he produced one in a week or so. It would be nice if all doctoral students proceeded with such speed and decisiveness. Few would hope to publish all three papers in top journals. They are crisp, elegant, and a joy to read.

This was Peter's first period, when he worked on economic growth models. His interest was already in optimality, in welfare judgments about the growing economy. His first papers added to the unfortunately large stock of impossibility results in economics. Following Tjalling Koopmans, that fine economist, who had already influenced him at Yale, he showed decisively and in great generality how it was impossible to establish principles for making welfare judgments that treated all generations equally and at the same time allowed comparison of any two growth paths.

Peter had great teachers: Tjalling Koopmans, and his three supervisors, Paul Samuelson, Bob Solow, and Frank Fisher. Following Solow he wrote about technical progress and growth; following Fisher he wrote about aggregation. Most significantly, he took Samuelson's finest paper, with its overlapping-generations model, and used it as the basis for a paper about the national debt in a growing economy, a paper that has become a classic. From general ideas about welfare, he had come closer to studying economic policy. Much of what he has done since has been about economic policy, and in recent years he has immersed himself in details of law and implementation, without ever losing the theoretical core. Indeed theoretical analysis remains central to his work, and powerful analysis it is too, as you will find in the lectures he is about to give in Munich.

The next paper of special note was not directly about economic policy. The subject was the stock market. It was work of great originality, opening up a theory of economies with incomplete markets. All economies have incomplete markets, as compared with the idealized picture of a general economic equilibrium, where everything has demand and supply, and prices allow demands and supplies to be equal. In particular, we lack anything like a full set of insurance markets. The stock market, as Peter modeled it, provides an imperfect and partial substitute. He made the first big step toward identifying and characterizing the imperfection; at the same time, he demonstrated a whole new set of problems that have to be addressed in properly describing the real market system.

This stock market paper has given rise, directly and indirectly, to a great deal of economics. So has his 1971 paper, modestly entitled "A Model of Price Adjustment." I jump ahead to that paper because, like the stock market paper, it represents Peter's long-standing interest in the economics of uncertainty, particularly the effect of uncertainty on the functioning of the market economy. This paper established rigorously, and in a particularly interesting way, the economics of search. In that paper, the notable result is that many independent firms in a market with search may behave as a single monopolist. It is a somewhat misleading result, but it highlights the importance of uncertainty. The idea of equilibrium as the outcome of a process where buyers and sellers search for one another is a fundamental one. Noneconomists may be surprised that economists have not always regarded the market economy in that light; but neither they, nor most economists, appreciated how great a difference the search account could make to economic outcomes.

Peter has developed the theory of search equilibria in many papers. They provide a persuasive basis for understanding macroeconomics, which is to say unemployment and inflation. It is a subject that rapidly becomes very difficult; and one is amazed how far he has been able to carry it.

Uncertainty is not Peter's only field. He has written more in public economics. It has been my great good for-

tune to share in that work—not all of it, but we have
written many papers together, starting more than thirty
years ago, first on optimal taxation, then on externalities,
on shadow prices, and on social security. Looking back
at them now, I find I rather like them, and I hope Peter
does too. Collaboration in economics, which is amazingly
common, can be either between complements or between
substitutes, to use economic jargon. I have done both, as
has Peter. Surprisingly, both kinds of collaboration can be
fruitful as well as enjoyable. Certainly Peter and I are not
perfect substitutes, but we are closer to that end of the
spectrum. I hasten to insist that, as any economist will
understand, being a substitute does not imply being just
as good. This collaboration has been one of the three best
things in my life. I do not know whether great minds
think alike, but this is the way to have a great mind to
think with.

Peter has done much that there is no time to tell you
about. His major work for many years now has been
on social security, and he will be talking about that here.
No one does it better. Before I close, I should tell you
about his abiding interest in other disciplines related to
economics—for many years, he taught a course on law
and economics. He has always been interested in psychology and has written a paper with Amos Tversky,
the psychologist. He has a number of deeply interesting
pieces, on social choice and methodology, that are philo-
sophically sophisticated. Even someone who gets up as
early in the morning as Peter cannot do everything he
would like to do. But he has also, wise man, found time to
see the world.

A good friend, and a good judge, once remarked that
Peter Diamond's papers were like good poetry. He may

also have said something about pearls before swine. Good poetry needs to be read and read again. It is worth it. It changes the way we see the world. It is with delight and pleasure that I introduce one of the finest economists I know, Peter Diamond.

James A. Mirrlees

Preface

I have analyzed social security systems on and off for twenty-five years.[1] Since social security became a major topic in the U.S. debate, I have been working more on than off this topic. Thus, when I received the opportunity and the honor to give these lectures, it was natural for me to turn to social security as their topic. The lectures were given November 14–16, 2000.

My goal for the first (public) lecture of this series was to illustrate how I approach some social security issues by analyzing some of the issues most relevant for the current discussion in Germany. My goal for the following two lectures was to present the backgrounds in subjects that influence my thinking about social security and then to show some applications to social security issues. For the book, I have rearranged the sequence of material, starting with the two technical lectures and dividing each of them

---

1. I use social security in the U.S. sense, as the public system of providing retirement income to workers. I was initially drawn into this topic by invitations from Bill Hsiao to serve on successive panels that he chaired, the Panel on Social Security Financing consulting to U.S. Senate Finance Committee, 1974–1975, and the Consultant Panel on Social Security of the Congressional Research Service, 1975–1976.

into three chapters. While expanding the material considerably, I have stayed fairly close to the lectures as delivered. I have moved the public lecture toward the end, with the written version in very much the same form as was presented. I have added a brief introduction, as a guide to the material, and a concluding chapter, where I review briefly some issues in the relationship between economic theory and policy recommendations.

One of the issues I faced was distinguishing these lectures from the Lindahl Lectures, which I delivered one year earlier.[2] There, too, I chose to consider issues of relevance in my host country. Then I turned to thinking about the interaction between social security and the labor and capital markets. These different approaches make the two books somewhat complementary, although it is inevitable that there is some overlap between them—in style and approach if nothing else.

For information and comments, I am indebted to Axel Börsch-Supan, Martin Hellwig, Jim Poterba, Emmanuel Saez, Andras Simonovits, Peter Temin, Jakob von Weizsaecker, Martin Werding, and especially Reinhold Schnabel. I also benefited from the comments of four reviewers arranged by The MIT Press. I am grateful to Tom Davidoff, Pavel Grigoriev, and Joanna Lahey for research assistance. The research reported on here was supported by the National Science Foundation, under grant SBR-9618698. The views expressed are my own.

I am grateful to Hans-Werner Sinn and his colleagues in Munich for showing me such a good and stimulating time during my visit.

---

2. Diamond (forthcoming).

Taxation, Incomplete Markets, and Social Security

1   Introduction

When I think about economic policy, I draw on my understanding of economic theory. Indeed, I draw on it in two distinct ways. First is the general underpinning of economic analyses that influences how economists approach questions generally. This underpinning includes both respect for the importance of incentives and awareness of the constraints that inhere in the notion of equilibrium. While these underpinnings are widespread among economists, my particular perspective also includes a large dose of second-best welfare economics, which is not so widely shared, particularly outside public economics. Second, when I think about specific policy design issues, I draw on models meant to illuminate specific economic forces that seem likely to be important for the questions at hand. This book is meant to illustrate how I approach some social security policy questions.

The book contains three very distinct types of chapters; introductions to parts of economic theory generally underpinning my approach, analyses of several formal models, and a discussion of some issues directly relevant for policymaking. I have tried to make each chapter self-contained even though they hang together overall.

Chapters 2 and 5 discuss critical general underpinnings for my thinking. Chapter 2 is an introduction to optimal income taxation, an introduction that is highly relevant since I analyze social security as a particular example of the approach of optimal taxation. While the chapter contains equations, the equations allow me to be specific about the models being discussed, rather than being bases for analytical reasoning. Chapter 5 discusses the incompleteness of markets (and contains no equations). These two chapters encompass two of the central underpinnings of my thinking about social security (which also reflects the inadequacy of individual savings decisions (Diamond 1977)). Chapter 2 highlights the impossibility of designing social security systems that do not have economic distortions. The goal, central to public finance analysis, is to portray the balance between distortions on one hand and providing insurance and raising and redistributing revenue on the other. Chapter 5 starts with the widely held awareness of economists who study insurance markets that these markets are very incomplete. This is in sharp contrast with, for example, many finance economists who study asset pricing while relying on an assumption of complete markets. Complete markets may (or may not) be an adequate basis for thinking about the prices of widely traded assets in organized markets. But complete markets do not seem an adequate basis for thinking about individual outcomes for workers, particularly for the large mass of families who have limited financial assets as they go through their life cycles.

Chapters 3, 4, 6, and 7 are totally different in style and intent. They contain models and analyses meant to illuminate particular facets of social security policy. While highlighting one issue, each of these models excludes other issues that also matter for social security policy. These simplifications are not meant to diminish the importance of omitted issues, but just to make progress in understanding by focusing on one issue at a time. Chapter 3 extends the widely studied one-period optimal income tax model to a two-period setting, one of work and one of retirement. Two questions are explored. One is the extent to which one wants to tax or subsidize savings, rather than relying on taxation (and retirement benefits) based solely on earnings. Second is the question of how the relative distribution of consumption among the elderly should differ from that when the elderly were young workers. That is, what pattern of consumption-replacement rates would occur at an optimum of this sort of model? Chapter 4 also considers this latter question. But it does so in a significantly changed environment— with an assumption that the labor supply decisions of the young are myopic, ignoring the effects of their current efforts on the retirement benefits they will receive when they are older. The two chapters together illustrate the effect on optimal policy of a change from assuming fully rational, forward-looking, time-consistent workers to assuming myopic, time-inconsistent ones.

Chapters 3 and 4 use models of varying skills, without variation in the length of working life. In contrast, chapters 6 and 7 consider why workers retire at different ages and how these underlying reasons should affect the incentives for retirement. This is analyzed in models where workers do not differ in their skills. Chapter 6 focuses on differences in the disutility of labor, while chapter 7 adds variation in the length of expected life. Both chapters find a role for positive implicit taxation of continued work beyond the age of earliest eligibility for retirement benefits. And both find that the return to continued work should happen not just in larger future benefits, but also in larger net pay while continuing to work.

In contrast with these discussions of underlying theory, chapter 8 is a discussion of issues directly relevant for policymaking, with a focus on issues of general interest that were of particular importance in Germany when I delivered these lectures in November 2000. As a public lecture, it is self-contained and math-free, in fact very close to the version originally presented.

Chapter 9 is a coda, discussing some issues in the relationship between economic theory and policy analysis. The discussion highlights the attention economists pay to incentives and their effects and the awareness of economists of general equilibrium and its constraints. The chapter also touches on political economy.

2   Income Taxation

Social security systems play a major role in how countries distribute income among the elderly.[1] Later chapters use the tools of optimal income taxation to make a start in analyzing the optimal design of a mandatory system for the provision of retirement income. This analysis builds on the considerable literature on the uses of income taxes to affect income distribution, a literature that has developed insights on how to balance redistributive gains with market distortions. Therefore, I begin by reviewing some of the income tax literature before adapting the models for consideration of social security. The central finding is that it is plausible that optimal tax considerations call for less dispersion of consumption among the elderly than among the young. I should note that the focus is on distribution within a cohort, and so subject to a single cohort-level budget constraint; that is, I do not consider overlapping generations issues.

---

1. In addition to explicit retirement income systems, many countries treat incomes of the young and old differently, with different income tax rules by age category and/or different income guarantee programs for the young and old.

Before turning to formal analysis of optimal income taxation, I want to start with the public finance perspective on the Second Fundamental Welfare Theorem.

2.1   Fundamental Welfare Theorem

Implicitly or explicitly, the fundamental welfare theorem plays an important role in policy discussions. The usual formulation of the second theorem is that any Pareto optimum can be achieved as a competitive equilibrium, provided that certain conditions are met and provided that income distribution is appropriate. It is unlikely that without government intervention the income distribution is right for some particular Pareto optimum, for example, the one that maximizes some social welfare function. Thus the second theorem is often stated as a need for the government to get income distribution right, but then no need for further interventions, provided the various conditions needed for the theorem are met (no externalities, convexity, competitive behavior). The equilibrium that occurs in this setting is a Pareto optimum and, therefore, has no distorting taxes, although it may have corrective (Pigouvian) taxes for externalities. Indeed, pointing out that some tax (or tax change) has (or increases) distortions or deadweight burdens, is a frequent part of policy discussions.

The starting place of modern public finance (to use the title of the Musgrave festschrift; see Quigley and Smolensky 1994) is that the lump-sum taxes needed for the theorem (varying person-by-person and independent of individual behavior) are not used in modern economies—indeed, are not available for use. Thus we have the public finance version of the Fundamental Welfare Theorem, based on the necessity of distorting taxes in order to have redistribution: *generically an optimized economy (with concerns about income distribution) has distorting taxes* (Diamond and Mirrlees 1971; Mirrlees 1986). Thus the problem is not to identify distortions but to describe the balance between distortions and improved income distribution. Measuring the magnitude of distortions is part of describing this balance, but only part.

The intuition behind this result is familiar. Consider an economy with no distorting taxes. The first (derivative) amount of distorting taxes has a second-order effect on efficiency (on deadweight burdens) (Debreu 1951; 1954; Harberger 1964; Diamond and McFadden 1974). But, unless changes in income distribution are assumed not to matter, introducing a derivative tax-transfer package has a first-order impact on income distribution (generically) and so a first-order impact on social welfare. The contrast between the first-order impact on income distribution and the second-order impact on efficiency implies that some distorting taxes would be part of any social welfare function optimum, generically.

Actually, there is a stronger public finance version of the fundamental theorem once one recognizes the necessity of tax revenue for the government functions needed for a modern economy (apart from a few resource-rich small countries). Some people do not have the capacity to earn the per capita cost of necessary government services. And there is asymmetric information on the ability to earn. Therefore, *even if one chooses to ignore issues of income distribution, it is impossible to have an equilibrium without distorting taxes.* There is still the question of selecting the set of distortions that is best. One can ignore income distribution and still formulate an optimization problem in terms of minimizing the aggregate deadweight burden, suitably defined. This problem has been addressed by Emmanuel Saez, whose paper (1999) I want to summarize

briefly. As does the Saez paper, I start with the familiar
Mirrlees (1971) model of an income tax that is contin-
uously varying under the full control of the tax author-
ities.[2] The underlying economic model is a two-good
model—consumption and labor.

2.2   Minimizing Aggregate Deadweight Burden

I begin by considering the standard Mirrlees optimal
income tax problem. This problem is to maximize the
integral over the population of the social evaluation of
individual utility. Individual utility, in turn, is a function
of the individual's consumption and labor. The maximization is subject to two constraints—a resource constraint and an incentive compatibility constraint. The
resource constraint is that spending on other public programs plus aggregate consumption be no larger than aggregate production. The incentive compatibility constraint
is that the utility of any individual be at least as large as
that if the individual chooses to earn the same income as
some other individual.

$$\text{Maximize}_{x,y} \quad \int_{n_0}^{n_1} G[u[x_n, y_n]] \, dF[n]$$

$$\text{subject to} \quad E + \int_{n_0}^{n_1} (x_n - n y_n) \, dF[n] \le 0,$$

$$u[x_n, y_n] \ge u[x_{n'}, n' y_{n'}/n] \quad \text{for all } n, n'. \qquad (2.1)$$

---

2. This is in contrast with models that have the structure of taxes restricted to a finite number of parameters (as in Diamond and Mirrlees
1971). Moreover, Saez works with a continuum of worker types in contrast with models with a finite set of worker types (as in Guesnerie and
Seade 1982; Stiglitz 1982).

Individual utility depends on consumption, x, and labor, y, with all individuals having the same utility function. Given the particular formulation of individual utility, u, G is a social cardinalization of the chosen representation of individual utility, reflecting social interpersonal comparisons. The social objective function is an integral of socially cardinalized individual utilities, integrated over the distribution of worker types. This additive structure can show concern for income distribution due to the concavity of G and u.[3] Workers differ only in productivity, denoted by n, which varies between n_0 and n_1. This is an important restriction, which has been weakened in some analyses. The resource constraint for the government is that government expenditures, E, plus aggregate consumption less production be nonpositive. Note the implicit assumption of a linear technology since we do not vary the productivity of a worker with the labor supply of other workers.[4]

The second constraint in (2.1) is the incentive compatibility constraint, given that the government does not observe the productivity of any particular worker. The government merely observes individual earnings and knows the overall distribution of skills. The constraint is that no worker would prefer to imitate the observable behavior (i.e., earnings) of some other worker. With one-dimensional variation in the population, this formulation

---

3. One could consider nonadditive structures, but the literature has not gone in that direction, apart from consideration of the Rawlsian max-min objective function.

4. The assumption is not important in a setting of complete taxation, such as this one, but would matter in settings of incomplete taxation, where changing relative prices have independent importance (see, e.g., Allen 1982; Carruth 1982; Diamond 1973; Feldstein 1973; Naito 1999; Wilson 1982).

in terms of comparisons is equivalent to one in terms of an explicit tax function as long as equilibrium earnings are monotonic in skill, as would follow from a normality assumption on preferences, which we make. In this problem, it is assumed that neither skill nor hours worked are observable. Since earnings are assumed to be observable, hours must not be observable if skill is to remain unobservable.[5]

Usually, analysis is done for the case of additive preferences:

$$u[x_n, y_n] = v[x_n] + w[1 - y_n]. \tag{2.2}$$

I focus on the further specialization to quasi-linear preferences:

$$u[x_n, y_n] = x_n + w[1 - y_n]. \tag{2.3}$$

This is an attractive example to consider for two reasons. Empirically, the income elasticity of the labor supply of prime-age males is close to zero, although income effects are important for both secondary workers and those in the range of retirement ages. In terms of theory, with quasi-linear preferences, the income derivative of labor

---

5. It is sometimes useful to rewrite the problem in terms of earnings rather than hours, leaving skill as the only unobservable variable. So, we denote earnings by z:

$z_n = n y_n$

In terms of earnings, we can rewrite the maximization problem as

Maximize$_{x, z}$ $\int G[u[x_n, z_n/n]] dF[n]$

subject to $E + \int (x_n - z_n) dF[n] \leq 0,$

$u[x_n, z_n/n] \geq u[x_{n'}, z_{n'}/n]$ for all n, n'.

supply is zero (given nonnegative income). This implies that Marshallian and Hicksian (or compensated) labor supply derivatives are the same, simplifying analysis. Also important is that changes in income level alone do not change labor supply or labor supply derivatives. This greatly simplifies the form of the first-order condition for optimal taxation, permitting straightforward interpretation. A major part of the difficulty in interpreting the solution to the general Mirrlees problem comes from possible changes in labor supply elasticity when average taxes but not marginal taxes change, as happens when marginal taxes have been changed on those with lower earnings. With this complication removed, understanding of the remaining elements determining optimal taxes becomes far easier.

This gives the Mirrlees problem the following form:

$$\text{Maximize}_{x,y} \quad \int_{n_0}^{n_1} G[x_n + w[1 - y_n]] \, dF[n]$$

$$\text{subject to} \quad E + \int_{n_0}^{n_1} (x_n - ny_n) \, dF[n] \le 0, \tag{2.4}$$

$$x_n + w[1 - y_n] \ge x_{n'} + w[1 - n'y_{n'}/n]$$

$$\text{for all } n, n'.$$

The standard approach to solving this problem, developed by Mirrlees, is to use the level of utility for someone with skill n, u_n, as a state variable and to replace the incentive compatibility constraints by a constraint on the derivative of utility, which coincides with local optimization:

$$\frac{du_n}{dn} = \frac{y_n w'[1 - y_n]}{n}. \tag{2.5}$$

The solution to this problem need not be the solution to the original problem because the constraint ignores the possibility that some workers would prefer to make large changes in labor supply. But this possibility can be checked. The optimum may have a range of workers of different skills having the same earnings and consumption. Ignoring this possibility of bunching of workers at some income level and also ignoring possible gaps in income distribution, this problem has the first-order condition for the optimal marginal income tax rate (Diamond 1998):[6]

$$\frac{T'[n]}{1 - T'[n]} = A_n B_n C_n,$$

$$A_n = 1 + e_n^{-1},$$

$$B_n = \frac{\int_n^{n_1} (1 - G'/\lambda)\, dF[n]}{1 - F[n]},$$
(2.6)

$$C_n = \frac{1 - F[n]}{nf[n]}.$$

This gives us an equation for the marginal tax rate, T', at the income level that is the equilibrium earnings for someone with skill level n, where e_n is the labor supply elasticity evaluated at the labor supply of a person with productivity n and λ is the Lagrange multiplier on the resource constraint. Given the lack of income effects, λ will equal the average of G' if it is possible to change the minimum level of income in either direction. However, if the minimum income cannot be lowered (for example, if it is

---

6. The derivation of this condition also makes use of the transversality condition.

equal to zero) then λ will not equal the average of G'.[7] This expression is easily interpreted intuitively. Raising marginal taxes at some income level has two effects. It increases the marginal deadweight burden at this income level, which depends on the labor supply or earnings elasticity at the income level where marginal taxes are raised, reflected in A. Raising marginal taxes at some income level transfers resources from all workers with higher earnings to the government, with a value captured in B. C gives the ratio of the importance of the two effects.

To explore the minimization of the aggregate deadweight burden (with no concern about income distribution), we can follow Saez and assume that G' is independent of the utility level where it is evaluated.[8] That is, with such a cardinalization, only aggregate

---

7. Following Saez (2001), we can give the first-order condition in terms of the distributions of earnings and virtual earnings rather than the distribution of skills, where virtual earnings are the earnings that would result in actual consumption given the linear approximations to the tax function at each earnings level. Both of these formulations are useful—the one in terms of skills for relating optimal taxes to underlying parameters, and the other in terms of earnings for relating them to directly observable variables.

$$T'[z]/(1 - T'[z]) = A_z B_z C_z,$$
$$A_z = e_z^{-1},$$
$$B_z = \int_z^{z_1} (1 - G'/\lambda)dH[z]/(1 - H[z]),$$
$$C_z = (1 - H[z])/(zh_v[z]),$$

where e_z is the elasticity of earnings with respect to the net-of-tax wage, H is the distribution of earnings, and h_v the density of virtual earnings. Now, we have an equation of the marginal tax rate at virtual earnings level z in terms of the elasticity of earnings with respect to the net-of-tax wage and the distribution of virtual earnings. An earlier formulation of the Mirrlees FOC in terms of elasticities is in Revesz (1989).

8. In the general case, it would be $G'u_x$ that would be assumed to be the same for all workers.

consumption plus the aggregate utility value of leisure enter the objective function. In this case, the optimal taxes become

$$\frac{T'[n]}{1-T'[n]} = \frac{(1+e_n^{-1})(1-G'/\lambda)(1-F[n])}{nf[n]}. \qquad (2.7)$$

Notice how the tax structure depends on the pattern of elasticities of earnings and the details of the distribution of skills. The latter can be inferred from the distribution of earnings. Saez has simulated the optimal tax structure given the skill distribution in the United States inherent in the distribution of earned income in tax reports and given an assumption that the elasticity of labor supply does not vary with skill. He does this for different levels of government expenditure needs and for different levels of the labor supply elasticity.[9] Also considering varying social marginal utility of income with consumption level, he finds an optimal structure of marginal tax rates that is U-shaped, as one would expect from the theoretical analysis in Diamond (1998). Greater expenditure needs raise the level of taxation, without changing the basic shape of tax rates. However, the issue of how elasticities vary with earnings level is one that is currently receiving attention (Gruber and Saez 2000). Having higher elasticities for very high earners tends to offset the effects leading to rising marginal rates toward the top. However, there is a major issue of interpretation of the elasticity given that high earners probably have more ability to do intertemporal substitution of realized income. It is the inter-

---

9. Assuming the government has an obligation to provide enough consumption for individuals to stay alive, this level of consumption replaces the zero consumption provided individuals with zero income in the earlier example. However, this can simply be incorporated in the level of expenditures E, leaving the analysis intact.

temporal government budget constraint that is relevant, not the annual one. There is also the question of how to incorporate changes in tax deductions (particularly charitable contributions and medical expenses) in the selection of elasticities to use for normative evaluations (Saez 2000c).

If one cares about income distribution in one's social evaluation, then there is a further argument for providing higher incomes for those with limited ability to earn, as opposed to zero or the minimum needed to keep people alive, in the setting of minimizing aggregate deadweight burdens. In turn, this higher income at the bottom of the income distribution requires raising additional revenue and is an argument for higher marginal taxes as the guaranteed minimum income is phased out. Moreover, declining social evaluation of individual income as one moves up the earnings distribution adds to the forces tending to make marginal tax rates rise at the top. High minimum incomes and high implicit taxes on low incomes is a feature of these solutions and of many government benefit programs.[10]

2.3 Annual Taxation

The Mirrlees model of income taxation is usually interpreted in terms of an annual income tax.[11] While the

---

10. This discussion has followed the Mirrlees assumption that the only marginal of adjustment to taxes is smooth—with the adjustment interpreted as hours of work or intensity of work. But in many circumstances, such as retirement, the relevant alternatives are discrete—for example, full-time work or no work. Discrete alternatives is also an issue for some low earners, given the fixed cost of work. This discrete choice of labor participation or not, rather than a smooth adjustment of hours, changes the nature of optimal taxation (Saez 2000b; see also Diamond 1980; Choné and Laroque 2001).

original analysis and further developments of the model
are insightful, they do not apply directly to actual tax
issues since annual income taxes recur year after year.
Recurring annual taxes are a complication because of the
links between incomes in different years—links that occur
because of savings, because of "human capital investments" that affect earnings in later years, and because of
the ability to adjust the timing of the realization of taxable
income. Thus, these issues arise with progressive taxation
even if one is trying to tax only labor income and not the
return to capital. An attempt to tax only labor income has
a further complication in that one cannot cleanly distinguish between labor and capital incomes. This point is
obvious for the self-employed who both work and use
capital in their businesses. It is also the case for ordinary
investors who devote time to trying to earn a higher (risk-
adjusted) rate of return. The potential to convert labor income into capital gains from stocks is another difficulty
with this approach.

In this chapter, I have ignored the taxation of capital
income and the use of labor input to affect returns on
capital—that would take us too far astray from the paral-
lels and links between payroll tax–financed social security
and annual taxation of income. I turn now from annual
income taxation to lifetime income taxation, starting with
the same model.

---

11. See, for example, Tuomala (1990).

3

Models of Optimal Lifetime Income Taxation with Time-Consistent Preferences

Unlike annual income taxation, social security systems look at earnings over much or all of a career. Therefore, one starting place for consideration of social security is to reinterpret the Mirrlees model as one relating the present discounted value of lifetime consumption to the present discounted value of lifetime earnings. Indeed, Vickrey (1947) has proposed such taxation, with taxes collected each year as a form of withholding for lifetime calculations that are not completed until death. Such an interpretation assumes that the interest rate is the same for borrowing and for lending and the same for all people, thereby abstracting from differences in investment ability and from the role of costs of investment that are not proportional to the amount invested. Moreover, in a lifetime context, the use of a multiplicative scalar earnings ability is more problematic as the only source of individual differences. In particular, length of career is important for lifetime earnings and relates significantly to disutility of work as well as to earnings ability. And, over a lifetime stochastic elements can affect both earnings ability and disutility. Moreover, such an interpretation relies on individuals to be time-consistent over their lifetimes.

Nevertheless, if we start by interpreting the Mirrlees model in lifetime terms, we preserve all the results that have been developed for an interpretation in terms of annual taxation. This gives us the same pattern of taxation relative to income as mentioned previously. Extending the model to a two-period model with one period of work (and so the same length of career for everyone),[1] one can consider the scope for more general taxation by taxing savings. This can be done by taxing first- and second-period consumptions differently, as in the many-good nonlinear optimal tax model, which has received a bit of attention (Mirrlees 1976, 1986), but not much. This is our starting place. Alternatively, if we assume that there is no savings, this becomes a model of earnings taxation in period 1 and benefit provision in period 2. Moreover, we can examine the question of whether consumption should be more or less equally distributed among the elderly than among the young. In this chapter, we explore these questions in the standard model of time-consistent full rationality. Chapter 4 explores optimal taxation in settings of less rationality.

This chapter begins with the setting of preferences separable between labor and consumption, where the optimum involves no taxation of savings (Atkinson and Stiglitz 1976). In this setting we compare the consumption distributions of young and old, finding conditions that sign the difference in equality of distribution between

---

1. More generally, in this chapter, the government is assumed not to make use of information about the time shape of annual earnings. Chapters 6 and 7 reverse assumptions—considering endogenous retirement ages but assuming that everyone has the same productivity. Chapter 7 also considers varying life expectancies, which are also missing in this chapter and the next.

young and old. Then, we examine two models where there is taxation of savings—a model without separability (Mirrlees 1976, 1986) and a model with heterogeneity in discount rates as well as skill (Saez 2000a). In the non-separable model, whether savings are taxed or subsidized depends on cross elasticities between labor supply and consumption in different periods. With the heterogeneous model, savings should be taxed with the empirically supported assumption that higher earners save a higher fraction.

With the present discounted value of lifetime earnings as the observable basis of taxation, the unobserved effort variable would reflect both intensity of work over time and the length of a career. But length of career is observable, an observability not used in taxation in this approach. We return to this issue in chapters 6 and 7, which consider retirement incentives, and so relate consumption to the length of career.

3.1   Income Taxation and Social Security with Retirement Age Fixed

As a start to thinking about social security from the perspective of what we have learned about income taxation, I consider a two-period variant of the Mirrlees problem presented in chapter 2. Assume there is work in the first period, with the usual choice of hours, but no work by anyone in the second period, with consumption occurring in both periods. In general terms, we would write lifetime utility as $u[x_n, c_n, y_n]$, where x is first-period consumption and c is second-period consumption. To begin, I focus on the case of separability between labor and consumption,

$v[x_n, c_n] + w[1 - y_n]$. In the course of this and the next chapter, I contrast three versions of such a model—with rational savings and labor supply, with rational labor supply and no savings, and with myopic labor supply and no savings. In all three versions, the normative evaluation is in terms of lifetime utilities, although I do not think that is an adequate basis for evaluation when workers are not time consistent in their choices. In particular it is not completely satisfactory to consider a concave transformation of lifetime utility for social welfare purposes when individuals do not behave in a time-consistent manner relative to consumption at different ages. The alternative simple approach of ignoring concavity in the social evaluation is mathematically convenient, but it loses concerns about income distribution that are captured in some measure by increased curvature in the social evaluation. That is, the question is the extent to which the social evaluation of the flow of utility of the old should vary with the levels of consumption they had when young. An alternative straightforward approach is to apply curvature to a social evaluation of period utility, separately period by period. Generally this is an issue that deserves far more thought than it has received. A similar issue arises in the social evaluation of consumption levels for people with different life expectancies.

If there are rational savings and rational labor supply and no binding liquidity constraints, then the timing of taxes and transfers is irrelevant. All that matters is the present discounted value (PDV) of the return to work. Thus, the standard Mirrlees model can be interpreted as applying to this two-period model. If we assume further that $v[x_n, c_n]$ has constant returns to scale, then utility is linear in income for lifetime consumption, and so the first-order condition looks just like that for the quasi-linear utility income tax problem in chapter 2.[2]

Basing taxes only on lifetime earnings implies that there is no differential taxation of consumption in the two periods. In this setting we can ask if welfare would be improved if there were differential taxation of consumption in the two periods. This question could be approached by having linear taxes on savings or by considering a more general nonlinear tax problem assuming that the government can measure consumption in each period.

If we assume a separable structure of preferences between consumption and labor and the usual model of one-dimensional differences in the population with differences only in productivity, then there is no reason to have different marginal rates of substitution between labor and each of the two consumptions in the two periods—the optimum would not use differential taxation of different consumption if that were an added policy tool (Atkinson and Stiglitz 1976; Mirrlees 1976). That is, with this preference structure, the optimum is indeed a tax based on the PDV of lifetime earnings, with no role for timing distinctions

---

2. A natural question to ask in this model is whether the optimum can be implemented by two income taxes, the same in each of the two periods, with income in the first-period being earnings less savings and income in the second period being retirement consumption. In general, of course, the answer is no, since people differ in intertemporal preferences and so have different ratios of first- to second-period consumption. A nonlinear tax on each of these is not equivalent to a nonlinear tax on the discounted sum. Even if everyone has the same ratio of second- to first-period consumption, the two separate taxes, the same in both periods, cannot mimic the overall tax unless the ratio is one. That is, with consumption-replacement rates different from one, the progressivity falls in different places in the two distributions.

inherent in social security.[3] However, if preferences are not separable, then one would prefer a more general tax function, depending separately on first- and second-period consumptions. Moreover, if we consider a population heterogeneous in both productivity and preferences, the optimum includes taxes on commodities, as has importantly been shown by Saez (2000a). For example, if, on average, people with higher productivity also have lower utility discount rates (and so tend to save more relative to earnings), there is a case for taxing savings. As Saez notes, this pattern is supported empirically in the United States.

We begin by formulating a model of general taxation. As with the two-good model, we let the government control all three variables directly, subject to the incentive compatibility constraints. This is equivalent to a potentially complex tax function. It can also be interpreted as a model where there are no private savings and so the government controls consumption in both periods through the taxation of earnings and the provision of retirement benefits. A natural next step, not explored here, would consider a two-types model with some people who do save and some who do not (with limited complexity of taxation). We begin by restating the optimization problem for general preferences—an extension of (2.1). The problem is to maximize the integral of the social evaluation of individual lifetime utilities subject to two constraints

---

3. This is similar to the public good analyses of Boadway and Keen (1993) and Kaplow (1996) that with an optimal income tax and preferences that are separable in a public good, the Samuelson first-order condition for public good expenditure with lump-sum taxation continues to hold. As with those results, the structure of preferences is critical for the result. The role of the interactions in preferences for taxation is an old issue, dating back at least to Corlett and Hague (1953).

—a resource constraint and an incentive compatibility constraint—that no worker chooses to earn the income planned for a worker with different skill.

$$\text{Maximize}_{x,c,y} \quad \int_{n_0}^{n_1} G[u[x_n, c_n, y_n]] \, dF[n]$$

$$\text{subject to} \quad E + \int_{n_0}^{n_1} (x_n + rc_n - ny_n) \, dF[n] \leq 0, \qquad (3.1)$$

$$u[x_n, c_n, ny_n] \geq u[x_{n'}, c_{n'}, n'y_{n'}/n] \quad \text{for all } n, n'.$$

For convenience, we repeat the notation:

G social cardinalization of lifetime utility

u lifetime utility

x_n first-period consumption of worker n

c_n second-period consumption of worker n

y_n labor supply of worker n

n productivity of worker n

E other government expenditures

r discount factor coming from production

As discussed earlier, in general, one would want to have implicit differential taxation of the two consumption levels, depending on the cross elasticities with labor supply. I begin with separable cases where this is not the case. That is, with separable preferences, the optimum has everyone with the same intertemporal marginal rate of substitution (MRS), which matches the intertemporal marginal rate of transformation (MRT). In this setting, I explore first the special case of fully additive preferences. Since everyone has the same intertemporal marginal rate of substitution at the optimum, this is equivalent to examining the pattern of savings in a setting of full rationality and taxation of the PDV of lifetime earnings.

3.2 Additive Case

We now write the utility function as additive in first-period consumption, second-period consumption, and leisure:

$$u[x, c, y] = v_1[x] + v_2[c] + w[1 - y]. \tag{3.2}$$

This preference formulation is commonly used in both theoretical models and simulations.[4]

As noted above, it is optimal to have the intertemporal marginal rate of substitution between x and c equal to the marginal rate of transformation for all n—there is no reason for inefficiency in consumption. One condition for optimality is therefore

$$\frac{v_1'[x]}{v_2'[c]} = r \text{ independent of } n. \tag{3.3}$$

Differentiating this expression, we can examine the pattern of retirement benefits relative to after-tax earnings when young. This pattern can be interpreted as the consequence of optimal taxes in the absence of private saving. Alternatively, and equivalently, the pattern can be interpreted as the outcome of individual savings decisions given optimal taxation of lifetime earnings (and no taxation of savings):

$$v_1''[x_n]\frac{dx_n}{dn} = rv_2''[c_n]\frac{dc_n}{dn} = \frac{v_1'[x_n]}{v_2'[c_n]}v_2''[c_n]\frac{dc_n}{dn}. \tag{3.4}$$

---

4. See, for example, Auerbach and Kotlikoff (1987).

Note the assumption that everyone has the same invest-ment opportunities (r does not vary with n). From (3.4), we can examine the pattern of the optimal consumption replacement rate, c/x, in terms of the degrees of risk aver-sion when young and when old.

Denote the indices of absolute and relative risk aver-sions by

$$A_i[x] = \frac{-v_i''[x]}{v_i'[x]} \quad \text{for } i = 1, 2,$$

$$R_i[x] = \frac{-xv_i''[x]}{v_i'[x]} \quad \text{for } i = 1, 2. \tag{3.5}$$

Then, substituting in (3.4), we have

$$A_1[x_n]\frac{dx_n}{dn} = A_2[c_n]\frac{dc_n}{dn},$$

$$R_1[x_n]\frac{dx_n}{x_n dn} = R_2[c_n]\frac{dc_n}{c_n dn}. \tag{3.6}$$

From the derivative of the consumption replacement rate and (3.6), we can relate the consumption replacement rate to the level of first-period consumption:

$$\frac{d(c_n/x_n)}{dn} = \frac{c_n}{x_n}\left(\frac{dc_n}{c_n dn} - \frac{dx_n}{x_n dn}\right)$$

$$= \frac{c_n}{x_n}\left(\frac{R_1[x_n]}{R_2[c_n]} - 1\right)\frac{dx_n}{x_n dn}. \tag{3.7}$$

We need to recognize that the indices of risk aversion are evaluated at different consumption levels. Thus we can conclude that if the retired have higher relative risk aversion than the young (both evaluated at optimal consumption levels), then the replacement rate is declining with the level of earnings, and therefore with skill.

$$R_1[x_n] < (>)R_2[c_n] \quad \text{implies} \quad \frac{d(c_n/x_n)}{dn} < (>)0. \tag{3.8}$$

This condition is stated in terms of endogenous optimal consumption levels. If the utility function is the same in each period, then the replacement rate is less than (greater than) one as the utility discount rate is greater than (less than) the real return on production. Combining this condition with an assumption on whether the index of relative risk aversion were rising or falling would determine the sign in (3.8). This determines whether there is more or less progressivity built into redistribution of the elderly relative to the young. Plausibly, utility functions do vary with age. Plausibly, the index of relative risk aversion of the elderly is larger than that of the young. Then there is less variation in post-retirement consumption than in pre-retirement consumption. Note that use of the same progressive income tax in each period is not likely to reproduce this pattern, even if pension savings is taxed on an EET basis—contributions and asset earnings tax exempt, with benefits taxable.

3.3   Quasi-Linear Case

While the additive case is familiar and is the two-period version of the widely used integral or sum of period utilities, neither familiarity nor wide use is really a justification for reliance on these preferences, since they do not appear empirically plausible. It is interesting to consider instead the case of linear Engel curves coming from homothetic preferences. For this purpose we assume constant returns to scale in consumption and that lifetime utility satisfies

$$u[x, c, y] = v[x, c] + w[1 - y] \quad \text{with } v \text{ having CRTS.} \quad (3.9)$$

Note that in this case the indirect utility as a function of lifetime income and leisure is quasi-linear.

Following the same logic as above, from the separability between labor and consumption we have

$$v_1[x_n, c_n]/v_2[x_n, c_n] = r \text{ independent of } n,$$

$$\frac{d(c_n/x_n)}{dn} = 0. \quad (3.10)$$

In this case, the replacement rate is constant and so social security is linear in terms of after-tax consumption. Even this case would not lend itself to repeated use of an annual income tax after a linear payroll tax unless the replacement rate were one. It would be interesting to explore other assumptions on preferences, reflecting both interaction between consumption in the two periods and greater risk aversion among the elderly.

3.4 Nonseparable Case

Mirrlees (1986) has examined the multigood problem without the assumption of separability. We consider a two-types version of optimal income taxation to visit his results in order to note the conditions that determine whether savings are encouraged or discouraged as part of the optimal tax structure.

We make a slight notational change, using the subscript i to mark the two types. We assume that type 1 has greater productivity: $n_1 > n_2$. We write social welfare maximization in terms of earnings, which are observable: $z_i = n_i y_i$.

With full nonlinear taxation, the equivalent problem to (3.1) can be written as follows:

$$\text{Maximize}_{x,c,z} \quad \sum f_i u[x_i, c_i, z_i/n_i]$$

$$\text{subject to} \quad E + \sum f_i(x_i + rc_i - z_i) \le 0,$$

$$u[x_i, c_i, z_i/n_i] \ge u[x_j, c_j, z_j/n_i] \tag{3.11}$$

$$\text{for all } i \text{ and } j,$$

where f_i are the fractions of each type.

With just two types, and the assumption that the only binding moral hazard constraint is type 1 considering imitating type 2 (high-skilled workers choosing to earn the same income as low-skilled workers), the problem becomes

$$\text{Maximize}_{x,c,z} \quad f_1 u[x_1, c_1, z_1/n_1] + f_2 u[x_2, c_2, z_2/n_2]$$

$$\text{subject to} \quad E + f_1(x_1 + rc_1 - z_1) + f_2(x_2 + rc_2 - z_2) \le 0,$$

$$u[x_1, c_1, z_1/n_1] \ge u[x_2, c_2, z_2/n_1]. \tag{3.12}$$

Forming a Lagrangian with the objective function minus λ times the resource constraint, plus μ times the moral hazard constraint, we have $\lambda > 0$ and $\mu > 0$. This gives six first-order conditions (plus the constraints):

$$f_1 u_x[x_1, c_1, z_1/n_1] + \mu u_x[x_1, c_1, z_1/n_1] = \lambda f_1, \tag{3.13}$$

$$f_1 u_c[x_1, c_1, z_1/n_1] + \mu u_c[x_1, c_1, z_1/n_1] = \lambda f_1 r, \tag{3.14}$$

$$f_1 u_z[x_1, c_1, z_1/n_1]/n_1 + \mu u_z[x_1, c_1, z_1/n_1]/n_1 = -\lambda f_1, \tag{3.15}$$

$$f_2 u_x[x_2, c_2, z_2/n_2] - \mu u_x[x_2, c_2, z_2/n_1] = \lambda f_2, \qquad (3.16)$$

$$f_2 u_c[x_2, c_2, z_2/n_2] - \mu u_c[x_2, c_2, z_2/n_1] = \lambda f_2 r, \qquad (3.17)$$

$$f_2 u_z[x_2, c_2, z_2/n_2]/n_2 - \mu u_z[x_2, c_2, z_2/n_1]/n_1 = -\lambda f_2. \qquad (3.18)$$

To examine the implicit marginal taxation of savings, we compare the intertemporal MRS with the discount factor from production. As usual with bounded skills, there is no implicit taxation for the highest skilled. Taking the ratio of the first two conditions (3.13) and (3.14),

$$\frac{u_x[x_1, c_1, z_1/n_1]}{u_c[x_1, c_1, z_1/n_1]} = \frac{1}{r}. \qquad (3.19)$$

Taking the same ratio for type 2, using (3.16) and (3.17), involves evaluating marginal utilities of consumption at different levels of labor supply:

$$\frac{f_2 u_x[x_2, c_2, z_2/n_2] - \mu u_x[x_2, c_2, z_2/n_1]}{f_2 u_c[x_2, c_2, z_2/n_2] - \mu u_c[x_2, c_2, z_2/n_1]} = \frac{1}{r}. \qquad (3.20)$$

If we had separability, then the ratio u_x/u_c would vary with x and c, but not with labor supply, z/n. In this case we would again get equality between the MRS and MRT. Generally, with $\mu > 0$, we have

$$\frac{u_x[x_2, c_2, z_2/n_2]}{u_c[x_2, c_2, z_2/n_2]} \leq (\geq) \frac{1}{r} \quad \text{as}$$

$$\frac{u_x[x_2, c_2, z_2/n_2]}{u_c[x_2, c_2, z_2/n_2]} \geq (\leq) \frac{u_x[x_2, c_2, z_2/n_1]}{u_c[x_2, c_2, z_2/n_1]}. \qquad (3.21)$$

Since the values at which the marginal rates of substitution are evaluated differ only in the level of labor supply, we have implicit taxation of savings (MRS < MRT) if the intertemporal marginal rate of substitution increases in labor supply. To consider the sign of this relationship, let us examine the derivative of the intertemporal MRS with respect to labor supply:

$$\frac{d}{dz}\left(\frac{u_x[x,c,z/n]}{u_c[x,c,z/n]}\right) = \frac{u_c u_{xz} - u_x u_{cz}}{n(u_c)^2} = \frac{u_{xz}/u_x - u_{cz}/u_c}{n u_x u_c}. \qquad (3.22)$$

Assuming the contemporaneous impact is larger (in percentage terms), we would expect that the absolute value of u_{xz}/u_x was larger than that of u_{cz}/u_c. But the expression is still ambiguous, depending on the signs of u_{xz} and u_{cz}.

3.5   Heterogeneous Preferences

Saez (2000a) has argued that workers with higher earnings save more relative to earnings, at least in the United States. This suggests that higher earners have lower discount rates. Again using a two-types model, we briefly review his argument to see how it results in a gain from taxing savings.

We now use separable utility (with the same function each period) but with different discount rates:

$$u^i[x,c,z/n_i] = v[x] + \delta_i v[c] - w[1 - z/n_i]. \qquad (3.23)$$

With full nonlinear taxation, and assuming that the only binding moral hazard constraint is type 1 considering imitating type 2, we can write the problem as follows:

$$\text{Maximize}_{x,c,z} \quad f_1(v[x_1] + \delta_1 v[c_1] - w[1 - z_1/n_1])$$

$$+ f_2(v[x_2] + \delta_2 v[c_2] - w[1 - z_2/n_2])$$

$$\text{subject to} \quad E + f_1(x_1 + rc_1 - z_1) + f_2(x_2 + rc_2 - z_2) \leq 0,$$

$$v[x_1] + \delta_1 v[c_1] - w[1 - z_1/n_1]$$

$$\geq v[x_2] + \delta_1 v[c_2] - w[1 - z_2/n_1]. \qquad (3.24)$$

The first-order conditions are as follows:

$$f_1 v'[x_1] + \mu v'[x_1] = \lambda f_1, \qquad (3.25)$$

$$f_1 \delta_1 v'[c_1] + \mu \delta_1 v'[c_1] = \lambda f_1 r, \qquad (3.26)$$

$$f_1 w'[z_1/n_1]/n_1 + \mu w'[z_1/n_1]/n_1 = -\lambda f_1, \qquad (3.27)$$

$$f_2 v'[x_2] - \mu v'[x_2] = \lambda f_2, \qquad (3.28)$$

$$f_2 \delta_2 v'[c_2] - \mu \delta_1 v'[c_2] = \lambda f_2 r, \qquad (3.29)$$

$$f_2 w'[z_2/n_2]/n_2 + \mu w'[z_2/n_1]/n_1 = -\lambda f_2. \qquad (3.30)$$

As in the previous case where everyone had the same (nonseparable) preferences considered above, there is no implicit marginal taxation of savings for the highest skill, as can be seen from the first two conditions:

$$\frac{v'[x_1]}{v'[c_1]} = \frac{\delta_1}{r}. \qquad (3.31)$$

From the two conditions for type 2:

$$\frac{(f_2 - \mu)v'[x_2]}{(f_2 - \mu(\delta_1/\delta_2))v'[c_2]} = \frac{\delta_2}{r}. \qquad (3.32)$$

If and only if $\delta_2 = \delta_1$ is there no taxation of savings for type 2. In the empirically plausible case, $\delta_2 < \delta_1$, then we have implicit taxation of savings for the low types. Similarly, if there is only linear taxation of savings (as analyzed by Saez), then savings should be taxed.

3.6   Conclusion

Considering the Mirrlees model on a lifetime basis opens up a number of issues. With the plausible assumption that the elderly are more risk averse than the young, optimal savings from a rational model with additive preferences would have low earners with higher savings rates than high earners. The counterfactual nature of this conclusion casts doubt on the empirical relevance of the many simulations that have been done with these assumptions.

4

Models of Optimal Lifetime Income Taxation with Time-Inconsistent Preferences

Social security is premised on the belief that many people are not doing the sort of lifetime utility maximization examined in chapter 3, but are making nonoptimal savings decisions (Diamond 1977). It is plausible, but basically unexplored, that if individuals are not paying adequate attention to future consumption when deciding on savings, they are also not paying adequate attention to increases in pension benefits as a consequence of higher earnings when deciding how much to earn.[1] That is, to what extent do young workers undervalue (or even ignore) implied increases in retirement benefits as a consequence of working harder and earning more. While the presence of time inconsistency requires serious thought about the choice of a social welfare function, I do not digress to do that.[2]

---

1. That labor supply of some workers may not adequately reflect future consumption gains is a likely source of the finding that replacing poorly designed DB systems by DC systems in Latin America did not have a significant effect on the labor market. Schmidt-Hebbel (1999) finds little impact except relatively in Chile, which also cut its payroll tax rate significantly, thereby making it impossible to separate the effects of the change in type of system from the change in tax rate.

2. For an analysis of social security with some examples of time inconsistent preferences and a discussion of normative criteria, see İmrohoroğlu, İmrohoroğlu, and Joines (2000).

Chapter 3 considered a model that could be interpreted as giving the optimal progressive earnings tax and optimal social security benefits for a model with no savings, but rational labor supply decisions. We saw that that could imply less inequality among the old than the young, but need not do so. We now contrast that model with one where workers are also myopic in their labor supply decisions. While there are interesting models based on quasi-hyperbolic discounting that derive the levels of saving (Laibson 1997) and retirement (Diamond and Koszegi 1999), a simpler approach is to assume that individuals do no saving. Similarly, I will consider the implications of having young workers simply ignore the impact of earnings on retirement income.[3] This analysis should be supplemented by having a two-types model where some people fit the rational model and some do not (for example, as in Feldstein 1985).

Assume that there is no impact on the labor supply decision of the response of future benefits to higher earnings. Then, the usual formulation of intertemporally additive preferences and no curvature to the social evaluation of lifetime utilities leads to the simple and stark conclusion that consumption of retirees should be uniform. Even more striking, with curvature to the social evaluation of lifetime utilities (with a lower social marginal utility of consumption for the elderly who had higher earnings and so higher consumption in the first period), pension benefits should decline with earnings. Of course, one can object on the basis that if young individuals are not paying attention to their later selves and if older individuals are not affected by what they consumed when younger,

---

3. The case of positive and age-varying awareness on retirement consumption would be interesting to explore.

the case for social welfare to pay attention to lifetime utilities constructed by adding up separate one-period utilities is weakened—a more complicated social evaluation is needed.

A second objection to the allocation result is that preferences are not intertemporally additive in the sense that the utility of the old does depend on the level of consumption they had when young—a standard-of-living effect. We therefore consider the model with myopia and a standard-of-living effect while making the plausible and very convenient assumption that there are no income effects on labor supply.[4] Moreover it is plausible that second-period consumption has a larger impact on second-period marginal utility than does first-period consumption. Then we would have optimal pension benefits that do increase with earnings, but less than one-for-one.

4.1 Two-Period Model, No Savings, and Myopic Labor

As previously, we write lifetime utility as $u[x_n, c_n, y_n]$, where x is first-period consumption, c is second-period consumption, and y is labor supply, and we focus on the separable case, $v[x_n, c_n] + w[1 - y_n]$.

Starting with the Mirrlees model in general terms (as in equation 3.1), changing the modeling of perceptions that affect labor supply means changing the incentive compatibility condition. Instead of perceiving changes in both first- and second-period consumption when contemplating having higher earnings, a myopic worker perceives a change in first-period consumption, but not

---

4. For analysis of optimal social security for a homogeneous population subject to disability risk with a standard-of-living effect in preferences, see Diamond and Mirrlees (2000).

in second-period consumption. Without additivity, one would need to select the level of future consumption that is part of the perception. With additivity, this term would drop out of the incentive compatibility constraint. A natural case to consider would have a worker correctly perceive the second-period consumption for the worker's own type, but not perceive a change in consumption if a different type were imitated. Thus the incentive compatibility conditions would differ. Instead of the constraint with lifetime perceptions being as written in (3.1):

$$u[x_n, c_n, ny_n] \geq u[x_{n'}, c_{n'}, n'y_{n'}/n] \quad \text{for all } n, n', \tag{4.1}$$

we would have a constraint with only first-period variation:

$$u[x_n, c_n, ny_n] \geq u[x_{n'}, c_n, n'y_{n'}/n] \quad \text{for all } n, n'. \tag{4.2}$$

This is a subtle difference in writing, but a major difference in behavior and outcomes, as we will see.

4.1.1 Additive Case

Let us start with the additive case. With myopic labor supply, retirement consumption does not enter the incentive compatibility constraint.

$$\text{Maximize}_{x,c,z} \quad \int_{n_0}^{n_1} G[v_1[x_n] + v_2[c_n] + w[1 - y_n]] \, dF[n]$$

$$\text{subject to} \quad E + \int_{n_0}^{n_1} (x_n + rc_n - ny_n) \, dF[n] \leq 0, \tag{4.3}$$

$$v_1[x_n] + w[1 - y_n] \geq v_1[x_{n'}] + w[1 - n'y_{n'}/n]$$

$$\text{for all } n, n'.$$

Since c_n does not enter the incentive compatibility constraint, the first-order condition (FOC) relative to c_n becomes

$$G'[v_1[x_n] + v_2[c_n] + w[1 - z_n/n]]v_2'[c_n] = \lambda r. \tag{4.4}$$

If G' were the same for everyone, then so too would be second-period consumption. More striking, if G is strictly concave, then those with higher earnings will have higher lifetime utility and so a lower value of G', implying lower retirement consumption. In this case, we would have a declining pension with skill and earnings.

4.1.2 Standard-of-Living Case

A different picture would emerge if we dropped the unrealistic assumption that preferences were additive over time. If we recognize that the utility from consumption depends on past consumption, then, even with a myopic labor supply decision, consumption after retirement might increase with earnings because consumption before retirement did.

We now assume that individual lifetime utilities for the purpose of social evaluation satisfy

$$u[x, c,] = x + v[c, x] + w[1 - y], \tag{4.5}$$

where the utility from consumption in the second period, v, reflects not just current consumption but also the history of consumption. An extreme example of such preferences would have only the ratio, c/x, enter into second-period utility of consumption.[5] We assume that

---

5. This function is explored in Davidoff, Brown, and Diamond (2001).

workers ignore the impact of work on second-period utility through both channels—directly through pension benefits and indirectly through the effect of first-period consumption on second-period utility. We assume that labor supply depends only on utility directly achieved in the first period, $x + w[1 - y]$.

From a labor supply point of view, we have workers maximizing what we will call *apparent utility*, a:

$$a[x, y] \equiv x + w[1 - y]. \tag{4.6}$$

We assume that the labor supply decision comes from a maximization of apparent utility and that there are no savings, with apparent utility quasilinear.

We now state the social welfare maximization, noting that retirement consumption does not enter the incentive compatibility constraint.

$$\text{Maximize}_{x,c,y} \quad \int_{n_0}^{n_1} G[x_n + v[c_n, x_n] + w[1 - y_n]] \, dF[n]$$

$$\text{subject to} \quad E + \int_{n_0}^{n_1} (x_n + rc_n - ny_n) \, dF[n] \leq 0, \tag{4.7}$$

$$x_n + w[1 - y_n] \geq x_{n'} + w[1 - n'y_{n'}/n]$$

$$\text{for all } n, n'.$$

From the definition of apparent utility, we can solve for first-period consumption:

$$x_n = a_n - w[1 - y_n]. \tag{4.8}$$

Then we can rewrite social welfare maximization, (4.7), as follows:

$$\text{Maximize}_{a,c,y} \quad \int_{n_0}^{n_1} G[a_n + v[c_n, a_n - w[1 - y_n]]] \, dF[n]$$

$$\text{subject to} \quad E + \int_{n_0}^{n_1} (a_n - w[1 - y_n] + rc_n - ny_n) \, dF[n] \le 0,$$

$$a'_n = y_n w'[1 - y_n]/n. \tag{4.9}$$

The FOC for c_n is similar to that above except that v_c, the partial derivative with respect to c, now depends on first-period consumption:

$$G'[x_n + v[c_n, x_n] + w[1 - y_n]]v_c[c_n, x_n] = \lambda r. \tag{4.10}$$

If G' is a constant, then, by differentiation:

$$\frac{dc_n}{dx_n} = -\frac{v_{cx}}{v_{cc}}. \tag{4.11}$$

It is plausible that $v_{cc} < 0$, and $v_{cx} > 0$. That is, second-period utility is concave in second-period consumption and higher first-period consumption raises the marginal utility of second-period consumption. Moreover, it is plausible that second-period consumption has a larger impact on second-period marginal utility than does first-period consumption. Then we would have c_n increase with x_n but less than one-for-one.

4.1.3   Special Case of Second-Period Utility Depending Solely on the Replacement Rate[6]

An extreme version of the standard-of-living approach is that only relative consumption matters:

---

6. Another interesting special case would be constant returns to scale for v.

$$v[c_n, x_n] = \phi[c_n/x_n], \tag{4.12}$$

with ϕ increasing and concave.[7]

The FOC for c_n is now

$$G'[x_n + \phi[c_n/x_n] + w[1 - y_n]]\phi'[c_n/x_n]/x_n = \lambda r. \tag{4.13}$$

Since $x_n + w[1 - y_n]$ and x_n are increasing in n, it follows that $\phi'[c_n/x_n]$ is increasing in n, implying that the replacement rate is decreasing in n.

If G' were a constant, differentiating (4.13), and using the index of absolute risk aversion for ϕ, A_ϕ, we would have

$$\frac{\phi''[c_n/x_n]}{\phi'[c_n/x_n]} \frac{d(c_n/x_n)}{dn} = \frac{1}{x_n} \frac{dx_n}{dn},$$

$$A_\phi[c_n/x_n] \frac{d(c_n/x_n)}{dn} = -\frac{1}{x_n} \frac{dx_n}{dn}. \tag{4.14}$$

Since ϕ'' is negative, the consumption-replacement rate would fall with first-period consumption level, and so with n. From the derivative of the consumption replacement rate, we have:

$$\frac{\phi''[c_n/x_n]}{\phi'[c_n/x_n]} \frac{dc_n}{dn} = \left(1 + \frac{c_n\phi''[c_n/x_n]}{x_n\phi'[c_n/x_n]}\right) \frac{dx_n}{dn},$$

$$A_\phi[c_n/x_n] \frac{dc_n}{dn} = (R_\phi[c_n/x_n] - 1) \frac{dx_n}{dn}, \tag{4.15}$$

---

7. The derivatives of ϕ and v then satisfy:

$v_c[c, x] = \phi'[c/x]/x$

$v_x[c, x] = -\phi'[c/x]c/x^2$

$v_{cx}[c, x] = -\phi'/x^2 - c\phi''/x^3$

$v_{xx}[c, x] = 2c\phi'/x^3 + c^2\phi''/x^4$

where R_ϕ is the index of relative risk aversion. The level of second-period consumption might rise or fall, depending on whether the index of relative risk aversion of ϕ is larger or smaller than one.

4.2   Optimal Tax Formula

Returning to the quasi-linear general model, $x_n + v[c_n, x_n] + w[1 - y_n]$, we consider now the optimal tax formula for first-period consumption (with the derivation in the appendix to this chapter).

Define the *apparent tax* as

$$A[ny_n] = ny_n - x_n. \tag{4.16}$$

As derived in the appendix, the FOC are

$$\frac{A'}{1 - A'} = -G'v_x/\lambda + \alpha_n \beta_n \gamma_n,$$

$$\alpha_n = 1 + e_n^{-1},$$

$$\beta_n = \frac{\int_n^{n_1} \{1 - G'(1 + v_x)/\lambda\} \, dF[n]}{1 - F[n]}, \tag{4.17}$$

$$\gamma_n = \frac{1 - F[n]}{nf[n]}.$$

In contrast, here are the taxes in the one-period quasi-linear problem presented in chapter 2:

$$\frac{T'[n]}{1 - T'[n]} = A_n B_n C_n,$$

$$A_n = 1 + e_n^{-1},$$

$$B_n = \frac{\int_n^{n_1} (1 - G'/\lambda)\, dF[n]}{1 - F[n]},$$

$$C_n = \frac{1 - F[n]}{nf[n]}. \tag{4.18}$$

If v_x were zero, then the first-order condition for first-period consumption would have the same form as the tax structure for the rational lifetime income taxation model, assuming that everyone consumes something in period 1. This follows from the quasi-linearity of preferences. With a constant marginal utility of first-period consumption, second-period consumption does not vary with earnings. Therefore, having individuals ignore second-period consumption does not change labor supply. The solutions to the first-order conditions are not generally the same since the government would choose second-period consumption differently than would a rational saver. That is, the social first-order condition

$$G'v_c = \lambda r \tag{4.19}$$

is generally not the same as the private first-order condition

$$v_c = r, \tag{4.20}$$

since G' varies with n in general. However, if, in addition G' is a constant, then, since retirement benefits would not vary, the two models are the same.

The additional term in the equation for the marginal tax rate is analogous to a Pigouvian tax correcting for an externality. In this case, the worker's decision process ignores the impact on the worker's own second-period utility, as measured by v_x. In addition, we have an extra term in the equation for β_n. Since the government can change income uniformly for everyone, the Lagrangian, λ, is equal to the average over the entire population of $G'(1 + v_x)$. It is plausible that G' is decreasing in skill. It is interesting to ask how v_x varies with skill. For this purpose, consider the special case where second-period utility depends only on the ratio of second- to first-period consumption, as in the previous example. Then, we would have

$$v[c_n, x_n] = \phi[c_n/x_n]$$

$$\frac{dv_x}{dn} = v_{xx}\frac{dx_n}{dn} + v_{cx}\frac{dc_n}{dn}$$

$$= (2c\phi'/x^3 + c^2\phi''/x^4)\frac{dx_n}{dn} + (-\phi'/x^2 - c\phi''/x^3)\frac{dc_n}{dn}$$

$$= \left\{ (2c\phi'/x^3 + c^2\phi''/x^4) + (-\phi'/x^2 - c\phi''/x^3) \right.$$

$$\left. \times \left(1 + \frac{c\phi''}{x\phi'}\right) \middle/ \left(\frac{\phi''}{\phi'}\right) \right\} \frac{dx_n}{dn}$$

$$= \left\{ \phi''(2c\phi'/x + c^2\phi''/x^2) + \phi'(-\phi' - c\phi''/x) \right.$$

$$\left. \times \left(1 + \frac{c\phi''}{x\phi'}\right) \right\} \frac{dx_n}{dn} \middle/ (x^2\phi'')$$

$$= \{(R_\phi)^2 - R_\phi - 1\}(\phi')^2 \frac{dx_n}{dn} \middle/ (x^2\phi''), \qquad (4.21)$$

where R_ϕ is the index of relative risk aversion for the function ϕ. The sign of this derivative depends on the size of the index of relative risk aversion, with large indices resulting in a decreasing pattern of v_x with skill. The critical value of R_ϕ where dv_x/dn is zero is approximately 1.6.

The extreme picture of retirement benefits comes from the absence of all effects, rather than a lesser effect, for example, from very high discounting. A more plausible structure would have some effect of future consumption on the incentive compatibility constraint, possibly some recognition of the effect of first-period consumption on second-period marginal utility, and a recognition that people with the same consumption-replacement rate have higher utility if they have higher consumption. In addition, this issue is also a candidate for analysis in a two-type model—with both forward-looking and myopic retirement decisions.

4.4   Concluding Remarks

A two-period model is highly limited for showing effects of changing ages. In a model with more periods, one could allow perceptions to vary by age and examine the effects of weighting different years differently in the benefit formula. In this way, one could also approach questions of benefit design and not just benefit progressivity. Note that this analysis has been done without recognizing variation in life expectancy—an important issue if one is considering a strictly concave social evaluation of lifetime utilities. The bottom line from these models is the suggestion that consumption among the elderly should be less dispersed than among the young. This would not be accomplished by a social security system where benefits were proportional to lifetime earnings.

Appendix: Quasi-Linear Model

We can write the problem as follows:

$$\text{Maximize}_{a,c,y} \quad \int_{n_0}^{n_1} G[a_n + v[c_n, a_n - w[1 - y_n]]] \, dF[n]$$

$$\text{subject to} \quad E + \int_{n_0}^{n_1} (a_n - w[1 - y_n] + rc_n - ny_n) \, dF[n] \leq 0,$$

$$a_n' = y_n w'[1 - y_n]/n. \tag{4A.1}$$

We can form the Hamiltonian

$$H = \{G[a^n + v[c_n, a_n - w[1 - yn]]] - \lambda(a_n - w[1 - y_n]$$

$$+ rc_n - ny_n)\}f[n] + h[n]y_n w'[1 - y_n]/n. \tag{4A.2}$$

For the first-order conditions, we have a as a state variable, so that $h'[n] = -(dH/da)$ and y as a control variable so that $dH/dy = 0$.

$$h'[n] = -\{G'(1 + v_x) - \lambda\}f[n]$$

$$\{-G'v_x w' - \lambda(n - w')\}f[n] = h[n](w' - y_n w'')/n \tag{4A.3}$$

Integrating and noting that the Lagrangian is zero at the top of the skill distribution, we have

$$h[n] = \int_n^{n_1} \{G'(1 + v_x) - \lambda\} \, dF[n]. \tag{4A.4}$$

Define the tax and apparent tax as

$$T[ny_n] = ny_n - x_n - rc_n,$$

$$A[ny_n] = ny_n - x_n. \tag{4A.5}$$

The individual FOC satisfies

$$w' = n(1 - A'[ny_n]).\tag{4A.6}$$

Therefore the social welfare FOC is

$$\{-G'v_x w' - \lambda(n - w')\}f[n] = h[n](w' - y_n w'')/n$$

$$\{-G'v_x w' - \lambda(nA')\}f[n] = h[n]n(1 - A')$$

$$\times (1 - y_n w''/w')/n$$

$$\{-G'v_x n(1 - A') - \lambda(nA')\}f[n] = h[n](1 - A')(1 - e_n^{-1})$$

$$-G'v_x/\lambda - A'/(1 - A') = h[n](1 - e_n^{-1})/\lambda nf[n],\tag{4A.7}$$

where e is the labor supply elasticity. Thus we have

$$A'/(1 - A') = -G'v_x/\lambda + \alpha_n \beta_n \gamma_n,$$

$$\alpha_n = 1 + e_n^{-1},$$

$$\beta_n = \int_n^{n_1} \{1 - G'(1 + v_x)/\lambda\}\, dF[n]/(1 - F[n]),$$

$$\gamma_n = (1 - F[n])/nf[n].\tag{4A.8}$$

5   Incomplete Markets and Social Security

In chapter 2 I argued that from the perspective of taxation, competitive equilibrium without distorting taxes was generically nonoptimal. Indeed, I demonstrated that an equilibrium without distorting taxes was not feasible. In this chapter, I turn to some issues of risk-sharing, which include both incompleteness of the set of widely available risk-sharing trade opportunities and incompleteness in the use of available opportunities. In parallel to the reversal of the fundamental welfare theorem when there are not ideal lump-sum taxes, so, too, we have a reversal *with incomplete markets: Generically, the competitive allocation is not Pareto optimal* (Geanakoplos 1990; Magill and Quinzii 1996).

There are interesting analyses focusing on the incompleteness of organized markets, particularly the incompleteness that accompanies an overlapping-generations perspective on risk sharing (Gale 1990; Bohn 1997). While this literature on trades that individuals can not make is very interesting, I focus on the available trades that individuals can but do not make, particularly their extremely limited use of annuity markets. Just as social security is

needed because many workers would not save enough for
retirement, so too social insurance is needed because
many workers would not adequately insure both risks to
future earnings and the risk inherent in a variable length
of life.

The focus of this chapter, and the modeling in the next
two chapters, is on an unmarried worker. This focus is
leaving out interactions within a couple. On the one hand,
Kotlikoff and Spivak (1981) and Brown and Poterba (2000)
have shown how risk sharing between husband and
wife decreases the importance of annuitization. On the
other hand, there is evidence that male workers do not
pay adequate attention to the potential financial position
should their wives outlive them (Holden and Zick 1998).
Indeed, in chapter 8 I argue that German social security
does not have a good pattern of survivor benefits for
elderly survivors, an argument that I have also made
for Italy and Sweden (Diamond 1999b, forthcoming) and
that many analysts have made for the United States (e.g.,
Burkhauser and Smeeding 1994; Diamond 1997). More
generally, considerable evidence exists that many families
do not act as if their behavior were equivalent to a single
(family) lifetime utility maximization and a small literature exploring behavior within the couple from a game-
theoretic perspective.

5.1   Incomplete Markets

Some transactions are organized in markets where one
does not know with whom one is trading. But trade in
most commodities occurs pairwise. Much pairwise trade
involves standardized commodities, available possibly at
multiple outlets. Other pairwise trade is individualized—

whether it is a made-to-order suit[1] or individualized insurance through friends or family[2] or arranged through Lloyds. Individuals do not purchase most of the standardized commodities that exist. And they do not partake in many of the individualized trades that they might make. So there are two interacting phenomena: the extent of availability of standardized products (or wide availability of possible trading partners pairwise) and the extent of use of these "markets."

The extent of availability of standardized products is dependent on the extent to which individuals are interested in the products. Thus there is an interaction between the availability of standardized products and the market participation of economic agents. For example, Shiller (1993) has argued for the risk-sharing advantages of markets in financial derivatives based on various indices. For example, trade in regional house price indices would permit people to hedge the risk in relative housing costs associated with strong reasons to move from one housing region to another. Or indices of wages by industry would let workers hedge the risk to the demand for labor in the industry, while still preserving the incentive to do well and be paid well. But an organized exchange in such derivatives would need a sufficient volume of transactions to make creation of such a market worthwhile. Many homeowners and workers would not participate in such markets. And those who would participate are likely to buy and hold, and so not contribute much to the volume of transactions that would make such a market liquid.

---

1. I am indebted to Stavros Panageas for drawing my attention to the relevance of this distinction.

2. See, for example, Ben-Porath (1980) and Kotlikoff and Spivak (1981).

Individuals do not make many detailed arrangements for the distant future. And they do not make many arrangements that distinguish among low-probability events. Thus, the Arrow-Debreu model with a complete set of markets is very wide of the mark relative to the extent of trading that does take place. As Foley (1970) and Hahn (1971) have noted, any fixed costs of arranging trades will result in rational agents choosing not to make some transactions—those sufficiently in the future relative to the discount rate and those with sufficiently low probabilities. And that, in turn, implies that in the future there will be opportunities for new trades, opportunities that would not arise if markets had been complete and trades had been executed over the full range of opportunities.[3]

The literature on incompleteness takes two forms. Some of the literature assumes full participation in the markets that exist and explores the implications of incompleteness of markets. Particularly interesting is incompleteness where the set of available trades is endogenous because relative prices are endogenous. Some of the literature focuses on limited participation in a given set of markets, a set that might even be complete. I briefly review the central insights of the first set of models, and then turn to nonparticipation—focusing on the reasons that individuals do not participate in particular markets.

---

3. The complete market Arrow-Debreu allocation can be achieved with fewer markets by complete trade in Arrow securities followed by trade in commodities once the state of nature is realized (Arrow 1963–1964). However, this approach still runs afoul of the Foley-Hahn objection to trade for sufficiently distant times and sufficiently low-probability events. Moreover, the Arrow argument requires perfect prediction of relative prices conditional on the state of nature despite the absence of markets that would provide that information.

The presence of an incomplete set of perfectly competitive markets has two implications. First, the markets give all participants the opportunity to equalize their marginal rates of substitution between each pair of (composite) commodities that are competitively traded, but marginal rates of substitution between commodities not separately traded are not generally equalized (Diamond 1967). Second, and more subtle and more interesting, is that variation in future endogenous prices affects current trading opportunities for future outcomes, resulting in the endogeneity of trading opportunities (Hart 1975). This endogeneity, in turn, implies that generically such a competitive equilibrium is not Pareto optimal relative to the interventions that a government could do without violating the information restrictions consistent with the market structure. Redistributing income or changing production plans today changes future relative prices and so changes current trading opportunities in assets where the payoff is dependent on future prices. Generically there is some redistribution and some change in plans such that the resulting change in equilibrium is a Pareto gain.

Given the set of markets that do exist, some individuals may not participate in the markets, even though their net demand would not be zero if they did participate. As noted above, intergenerational risk sharing through markets is limited to the set of generations that overlap. Similarly, in models with strictly rational agents, the presence of a fixed cost of participating in a market can lead some individuals to choose not to participate. Limited participation can affect the characteristics of the goods being traded (e.g., the volatility of the stock market depends on the number of people trading). Thus, with endogenous participation, more participation might well raise a social

welfare function or even be a Pareto improvement, because of the positive feedback of the degree of participation on the value of participation (Chatterjee 1988;
Pagano 1989). These normative possibilities are readily
seen in models with multiple equilibria that are Pareto
comparable.

5.2   Life Insurance and Annuitization

These models assume standard rational decisions about
participation. But, failures to understand the properties of
insurance and other psychological barriers to purchasing
insurance lead to some underuse of insurance (Kunreuther and Slovic 1978).[4] We can relate incomplete use of
available trades to transactions costs in a physical sense
and/or to decision failures. The latter include the cost of
genuinely learning about the product at hand. If this cost
is large (and learning may not be feasible for some), then
one can view incomplete use either as a decision failure or
as a transaction cost. But it may not be helpful to think in
terms of transaction costs when the concept of decision
failures links to the thinking that some people do and the
kinds of decisions that some people make. The cognitive
psychology literature has documented the fact that many
properties of random variables are not intuitive (Kahneman, Slovic, and Tversky 1982). This leads readily to decision failures in some contexts. It does not seem helpful
to lose this connection and think instead in terms of the

4. I ignore the tendency of some individuals to purchase insurance
policies that do not seem to make sense. Purchasing policies covering
small losses appears to make little sense. If individuals are sufficiently
risk averse to cover loads for small losses, their risk aversion for large
losses would be massive (Rabin 2000; Rabin and Thaler 2001).

categories of transactions costs. In the formal models below, I assume that certain trades simply do not happen, without necessarily deriving the nontrading behavior from a particular underlying cause. For many positive and normative issues, the findings should be robust to cause; for others, they should not, and one needs a more complex analysis.

It would be natural to start consideration of annuities in their most common form—contracts that last for an entire remaining lifetime and have some particular intertemporal structure. Instead, I want to start with an annuity as a special example of an Arrow security.[5] This will be closer in spirit to the argument in Yaari (1965), who bases his analysis on a complete market Arrow-Debreu competitive equilibrium and is the source of the widely cited result that individuals without an interest in bequests, with access to actuarially fairly priced insurance, and without other risks should annuitize all of their wealth.

An Arrow security pays off at a particular time in a single state of nature. Let us consider the special case where a single individual's mortality risk is the only risk in the economy. It is easy to generalize afterward. Then, at each point in time the individual is either alive or dead. (I ignore the relevance of history up to the time of death for mortality probabilities.) If we have complete markets, the individual can purchase separately income at each time conditional on being alive and conditional on being dead. Purchase of a conventional zero-coupon bond of some maturity means purchasing equal amounts of the two contingent commodities for that point in time. By the arbitrage condition, we know that the cost of a unit of

---

5. This approach is also taken in Davidoff, Brown, and Diamond (2001).

unconditional consumption at that time equals the sum of
the costs of the two conditional consumptions. If an individual has no bequest motive, then income conditional on
being alive is as good for the consumer as an unconditional payment. The only way an individual would not
annuitize all of the wealth being used to purchase consumption for that time is if it is not cheaper to purchase
the conditional consumption. But as long as there is a
positive probability of being dead, and as long as the
transaction cost of delivering conditional consumption is
not too much larger than the cost of delivering unconditional consumption, then the annuitized income provides
a dominant asset. This is the logic behind the Yaari result.
It is clear that it extends to a complete market Arrow-
Debreu setting with lots of additional risks as a statement
comparing payments that distinguish other risks and do
or do not distinguish whether the individual is alive. This
argument holds for insurance that need not be actuarially
fair as long as contingent income is cheaper than non-
contingent.[6]

Next, consider the analysis when some people do value
income even if dead, perhaps because of family members.
Individuals can contract separately for income if they are
dead or income if they are alive. The former is life insurance, although payoffs are usually triggered by dying
rather than being conditional on being dead. But that is a
small difference.[7] Income if alive has a less familiar form.

---

6. For some results that hold with incomplete markets, see Davidoff,
Brown, and Diamond (2001).

7. There is bundling of some life insurance products in that a payoff on
dying is made over a range of dates when the death might occur. If the
life insurance were paid as an annuity to a survivor, it would be closer to
the theoretical structure.

We are familiar with annuities that pay a flow of income for the rest of the time that a person is alive. The flow might be constant in nominal or real terms, or have some particular simple time shape (graded), or be conditional on the return on some particular portfolio (variable annuities). But if we decompose this flow into separate dates and possibly different amounts at different dates, we see that a standard annuity contract is a combination of Arrow securities, paying particular amounts at different dates in the event of being alive.

An individual contemplating some future date and holding some particular asset portfolio has a marginal rate of substitution between income if alive and income if dead at that date. For an active worker with dependents, in the absence of any insurance, there is likely to be higher marginal utility for income when dead (relative to its price as fair insurance). Or someone with no dependents might have a clear preference for income if alive (given an actuarially fair annuity). If pricing is fair, it would be a zero-probability knife edge that one did not want either life insurance or annuity coverage (Bernheim 1991). That is, without any insurance, there are equal wealth amounts in the two states. It would be unusual for this pattern of equalized wealths to result in a marginal rate of substitution that equaled the price ratio of the two types of insurance. With load factors on the two types of insurance, there is a kink in the budget constraint and some fraction of the population would be expected to be found in the position of no insurance of either kind. This pattern of outcomes is similar to that with borrowing and lending. If borrowing and lending rates are equal, we would not find many people deciding to do neither. With a higher borrowing than lending rate, some people will be at the kink in the budget constraint of zero borrowing and lending.

Study of the extent to which people purchase life insurance (Bernheim et al. 2001) suggests that many Americans with families are underinsured, as measured by the ability of the surviving family to sustain the same standard of living. And studies of the value of annuitization, even with simple annuities, find that the value is so large that it is surprising how little use people without dependents make of annuitization (Mitchell et al. 1999).[8] Even those with dependents would want to combine life insurance for some dates with some annuitized payouts at others.[9]

---

8. There is a sizable market in the United States for what are called "variable annuities." However, while these insurance products include an option to annuitize, they do not commit the investor to an annuity. Moreover, it appears that very few people saving in this form do purchase annuities.

9. Considerable annuitization happens around the world in three common forms. Private pension plans often provide benefits only as an annuity. Public mandatory pension plans often do too. Some tax-favored retirement savings plans require or strongly tax-favor some annuitization (U.K.). But, left to their own devices, individuals do very little annuitization. This suggests a role for public programs that encourage or require annuitization (such as paying retirement benefits as an annuity rather than a lump sum). To explore this issue, we need to consider why individuals might not annuitize. There are several reasons. One is that government programs provide sufficient annuitization. This includes both formally annuitized ones and ones that are annuitized in practice by being annual programs. This is an awkward line of argument. If the programs exist because individuals would not otherwise annuitize, then provision of considerable annuitization undercuts the ability to judge the need for annuitization. The lack of annuitization where government retirement programs are small suggests that government provision is not filling a role that the private market would fill otherwise. Second, we can consider the terms on which annuities are offered. If they are very expensive because of the high costs of administering them, then there may

The Yaari argument assumed actuarially fair insurance. But it is clear that the argument does not require actuarially fair insurance. For someone with no bequest motive (e.g., young and single), the argument just needs the result that the annuitized return exceed the zero-coupon bond return. Let us see how this might look in the more familiar setting of household financial investment. The sense in which an annuity is a dominant asset for someone with no bequest motive becomes clear if one contemplates a short period investment opportunity with the properties of a TIAA-CREF annuity (Valdes-Prieto 1998). Consider investing in some mutual fund or a bank certificate of deposit (CD) for a given time period (a year or a month). Consider instead investing in the same mutual fund or CD with the condition that the accounts of all the people who die during the investment period are divided proportionally among the accounts of the survivors. If one does not value resources after death, the annuitized mutual fund or CD is a dominant asset as long as the administrative cost of determining death and reapportioning the accounts does not exceed the value of the accounts freed up by death. One does not need a long time horizon for such an investment opportunity to be a dominant asset. Thus it is interesting that such given horizon investment

---

not be much role for them. However, as I will argue, the costs need not be high and much of the high costs come from consumer behavior. Indeed, high selling costs because of the need to convince people to annuitize suggest that the market does not function smoothly. I pass over for now the consistent track record that the government can provide insurance more cheaply than the market can (Beveridge 1943). This leaves us with two reasons based on consumer behavior. Either consumers do not have an advantage from annuities or consumers are not making good decisions because of failures to appreciate and take advantage of the nature of annuities.

opportunities do not exist.[10] Presumably this reflects companies not offering what they believe the public is not ready to purchase, at least without a selling campaign that would be too costly to be justified. Note that with this plan the supplier does not take on any risk from mortality. But this analysis suggests strongly that the determination of such behavior does not lie in consumer costs of participation, since the potential gains are large. As noted previously, one does not need risk classification for this to be a dominant asset. While I would prefer to be grouped with people with a high probability of dying, being grouped with people who have any positive probability of dying is sufficient for this to dominate as an asset (for sufficiently low additional administrative costs).

This result does depend on the richness of alternative annuity payout streams. If individuals are restricted to some particular class of annuities, such as constant real payments for the rest of life, then the inefficiency in the shape of the stream might lead some to hold unannuitized wealth. Yet the simpler structures would be easy to administer. And they would permit people to divide their wealth between traditional mutual funds and annuitized mutual funds, and so have whatever different relative amounts of wealth conditional on survival or not. That these simple financial instruments do not exist indicates strongly that there is no demand for them, a lack of demand that suggests that people do not appreciate the potential in this type of insurance. A further argument for limited understanding comes from the annuities that peo-

---

10. If they did exist, it would be natural for providers to try to draw distinctions in risk classes. With risk classification, then one would not get insurance against one's future risk classification merely by rolling over short-term purchases.

ple do buy. It is common for annuities to come with a guarantee of some minimum payout. This is a peculiar form of bequest since it is random and purchase of an annuity without such a guarantee would permit a non-stochastic bequest and the same level of annuitized income flow.[11]

Another issue that arises in the limited uses of annuity markets that do occur relates to the timing of annuitization. People tend to accumulate sums and then purchase an annuity late in life. Yet this exposes an individual to risk of how they will be classified by insurance companies for annuity purchase. That risk can be avoided by purchasing the annuity early, before the arrival of news that determines the placement in whatever risk classification scheme exists (Brugiavini 1993; Sheshinski 1999). It also does not convert wealth in the state of dying before retirement into higher retirement benefits conditional on surviving to retirement. Defined benefit pensions take care of these problems by having uniform risk classification (uniform relationship between earnings history and benefits) and by paying benefits to workers who survive to retirement age (although there may also be life insurance benefits as well).[12]

Thus we have another role for social insurance—providing insurance that the market does not provide, perhaps because individuals do not appreciate its virtues. Annuitization is central in the design of defined benefit

---

11. Also at odds with rational modeling is the popularity of nominal annuities among annuity purchasers. Presumably, this reflects limited understanding of inflation processes (Shafir, Diamond, and Tversky 1997). More generally, economists are very aware how limited the demand for inflation indexed bonds is in most countries.

12. While DB pensions handle this risk issue, they distort the incentive for labor supply (Diamond, forthcoming).

pensions systems without lump-sum payout options. Insuring the length of one's career (Diamond and Mirrlees 1978, 1986, 2000, forthcoming) or one's earnings trajectory (Dulitzky 1998) is another opportunity for a system basing benefits on lifetime earnings records, although it should be recognized that an annual income tax provides some of this insurance by itself.

I conclude that failures to annuitize, like failures to save for retirement, represent a consumer failure that government intervention could potentially improve. This is an argument for the justification of intervention that is separate from one based on adverse selection issues. The difference leads to different ways of modeling individual behavior and therefore possibly different descriptions of optimized interventions. The next question is to analyze how such interventions might be organized and what implications follow from the form of realistic intervention, if well executed.

Mandating some savings can help some people who do not save enough for retirement and save less than the mandate. However, it may hurt those who should save less than the mandate and may also hurt those who would have saved anyway and suffer from some of the restrictions or lost opportunities associated with the mandated savings program. Moreover, when the quantity of mandated savings is linked to earnings, then there is some implicit taxation of earnings associated with the mandate. The implications of that implicit taxation, along with any explicit redistribution, needs to be considered as part of the evaluation of the program.

When we turn to the form of retirement benefits, we have the further issue that full annuitization may be too much annuitization for some. A further issue comes with individuals with different life expectancies lumped into a single risk class for annuitization purposes. While the market has heterogeneous individuals in each risk class, the government use of risk classes is likely to be very different from that of the market. As a matter of principle, the government might choose to have a single risk class, ignoring all easily observable as well as expensively available indicators of life expectancy. A program with a single risk class redistributes to the longer lived compared to annuitization with separate risk classes. The comparison to a market outcome without annuities is more complex because of the gains from getting insurance. These gains and the redistributions across life expectancies together determine the pattern of gains and losses for this counterfactual. A program that is break-even for the entire population will be a subsidy of earnings for some and a tax on earnings for others. Of course a lack of annuitization, as a way to avoid this issue, has problems of its own. Restricting attention to workers with the same earnings potential, those who expect to live longer would, with the same preferences and career length, have higher marginal utility of consumption since they have more periods over which to spread the accumulated earnings.

In the next two chapters, we explore the design of optimal retirement incentives for a population with the same earnings level, but differences in the disutility of labor (chapter 6) and also life expectancy (chapter 7).

6   Models of Optimal Retirement Incentives with Varying Disutility of Labor

Chapters 3 and 4 considered redistribution across workers with different earnings levels, ignoring any variation in retirement ages. This chapter and the next reverse the focus—considering different possible retirement ages while ignoring variation in earnings levels. That is, on reaching the earliest age at which retirement benefits can be claimed, there is some level of benefits available for a worker with a given history of earnings.[1] The increase in benefits as a consequence of delayed retirement is the focus of attention, ignoring any effect such rules might have on earlier behavior. In principle, such adjustment for delayed retirement could be designed to vary by earnings level. In practice, systems have rules for determination of initial benefit levels and rules for determination of increases for delayed retirement that interact in limited ways. Thus there is a need at some point to put together the two aspects I am exploring in these lectures. But that will not happen here. I have two bottom lines. One is that for reasons of income distribution and insurance, there

---

1. I will not consider the interesting question of the selection of an earliest entitlement age, but just consider retirement incentives beyond that age.

should be some taxation of work for those eligible for retirement benefits—basically with the variation analyzed here, a long career tends to be correlated with lower social marginal utility of consumption.[2] Second is that the return to work should show up in both higher net earnings when working and higher later benefits for those who delay retirement, not just the latter.

Put differently, the pension system (along with the wage) determines the financial incentive to continue working despite eligibility for retirement benefits. In thinking about this incentive, I identify two issues: the cost of the financial incentive to continue working, and how that incentive is divided between current compensation and increased future benefits. I address both of these questions in a series of special models considering separately various reasons why different workers might retire at different ages. The analyses derive the optimal uniform system, not drawing any distinctions between public and private systems. This analysis ignores any presence of unemployment insurance or disability insurance programs covering the same ages.[3]

If there were perfect capital markets, if there were perfect insurance markets, and if workers were time consistent, it would not matter how the financial incentive for retirement was divided between current compensation and larger future benefits. But none of these three con-

---

2. I do not consider variation in retirement age due to differences in past savings behavior, previous access to private pensions, or inheritances received. Since an income effect is conducive to earlier retirement, this would tend to offset the argument from assumptions that lead to those with short careers having higher marginal utility of consumption. In general, the income tax literature has not paid much attention to this issue.

3. For analysis of disability and retirement programs together, see Diamond and Sheshinski (1995).

ditions hold in practice. First, some workers are liquidity constrained, and so prevented from using larger future benefits to finance additional current consumption. Second, future benefits are paid as an annuity. As noted by Crawford and Lilien (1981) payment as an annuity can be valued more highly than current compensation by some workers who would not otherwise have access to as good an annuity (or any annuity). And third, some workers are not time consistent in savings decisions, and so their consumption behavior may vary with the form of compensation. Moreover, workers with different life expectancies have different relative valuations between uniform annuities and lump sums.

With an assumption of time inconsistency in savings decisions, one can still model the retirement decision as rational given a correct forecast of savings behavior (after retirement), or one can consider a retirement decision that is also short-sighted in some form. Separate from individual behavior is the issue of how social welfare should evaluate individual decisions. The formulation of social welfare is obviously an issue when workers are not time consistent. It is also an issue when their behavior affects others, through bequests. It may even be an issue when workers are time consistent and leave no bequests if the social evaluation does not coincide with individual preferences because society concludes that the extent of discounting by the worker is not socially appropriate. This issue is further compounded if we are considering a couple, rather than a single worker. But I will not pursue the interesting and little developed issues of family behavior around savings, retirement, and annuitization.

This chapter analyzes models with three periods. This setup allows consideration of both ex ante heterogeneity and individual uncertainty (with an assumption of no aggregate risk). The first model is a three-period model, with variation in the additive disutility of labor being the only element of variation in the population. After considering this model with a forward-looking retirement decision, I consider the same model with myopic retirement decisions. Also summarized is some work I have done with Mirrlees with a stochastic end of working ability in a model of ex ante homogeneity. The next chapter adds varying life expectancy to the model with fully rational decisions in this chapter.

6.1   Variation in Retirement Ages

In countries with reasonable retirement incentives, a large spread in retirement ages exists—labor force participation rates decline over a range, not abruptly (Gruber and Wise 1999). First, I review why different workers might be retiring at different ages, given a pension system that does not induce everyone to retire at the same age. To do this, I set up a simple model of the portion of the life cycle coming after the early entitlement age, with a focus on the retirement decision for a nonsaving worker. Implicitly, I am assuming that the form of retirement system has no important implications for earlier behavior, or that someone else will extend the model to earlier ages. What may matter for earlier behavior, and what is held constant, is the level of resources accumulated by the early entitlement age and available for retirement benefits. I think that the particular pattern of incentives beyond the early entitlement age may not be too important for earlier behavior, at least not until a worker is close to the early entitlement age. After reviewing a broad model, a special case of the model is analyzed for optimal retirement incentives.

For notational convenience, I assume that both the interest rates earned on all accumulations and the discount rates of workers are zero. The substantive part of this assumption is that I ignore variation in utility discount rates in worker retirement behavior. Variation in utility discount rates is likely to be important for optimal policy, as it is for design of an optimal income tax (see the chapter 3 discussion of the model in Saez 2000a). In discrete time, the common model of worker lifetime utility in a certainty setting is

$$U = \sum_{z=1}^{R} \{u[x_z] - a_z\} + (L - R)v[c_R], \qquad (6.1)$$

where we have assumed that preferences are intertemporally additive, that period utility functions are independent of age (apart from an additive component of the disutility of labor), that work does not have an intensity choice variable, and that benefits are consumed as a constant real stream. We have measured time from the early entitlement age. This formulation uses the following notation:

a_z disutility of labor at age z

U realized lifetime utility

R retirement age

L length of life

n_z productivity at age z

c_R consumption per period after retirement at age R

x_z consumption at age z before retirement

$u[x] - a$ utility function before retirement, differentiable and strictly concave

$v[c]$ utility function after retirement, differentiable and strictly concave

This setup ignores an effect of labor intensity on disutility, treating work as a zero-one variable.[4] In designing a pension plan, the realized net cost of benefits for this worker is

$$C = \sum_{z=1}^{R} \{x_z - n_z\} + (L - R)c_R. \tag{6.2}$$

The formal analysis to follow assumes that productivity, n, does not vary with age, nor across the population. The preference parameters that can vary across the population in a certainty setting are then disutility and length of life. Disutility is presumed not to be observable. And length of life becomes revealed, although expected length of life is not observable. This chapter focuses on variation in disutility, while chapter 7 focuses on length of life.

With the population identical ex ante, uncertainty can be added in this simple setting by assuming that productivity becomes zero stochastically, or that equivalently, disutility becomes infinitely high. I have explored this model in a series of joint papers with Mirrlees, which I summarize later in this chapter. Making length of life stochastic (with identical workers ex ante) is a minor modification if there is full annuitization. A stochastic length of life with ex ante variation and alternative institutional structures is the focus of chapter 7. More complications, particularly keeping track of what is happening in the model, would combine age-varying patterns with sto-

---

4. This makes productivity observable for those who work, but not for those who are retired, an issue that is ignored here. The change in optimal income tax from this change in assumptions has been examined in Diamond (1980), Saez (2000b), and Choné and Laroque (2001).

chastic elements. For example, people could be learning more about their mortality rates as they age.[5]

This chapter analyzes models with three periods. This setup allows consideration of both ex ante heterogeneity and individual uncertainty (with an assumption of no aggregate risk). The common message in these models is that taxing work beyond the early entitlement age is part of optimal insurance and optimal redistribution. Moreover, when there is no saving, the compensation for work should take the form of adding to both current compensation and future benefits, not just one or the other.

Let me describe how this might work in practice (which is a proposal I made for the United States nearly twenty years ago, based on my work with Mirrlees, and a belief it would carry over to more models). Starting at the early entitlement age, part of benefits is paid independent of retirement and part is paid only if the worker retires. The two fractions shift with age. Delayed benefits are increased to partially offset the expected loss in income from withholding part of benefits. Administratively, such payments would be easy in a system that has a retirement requirement for benefits, but would be an administrative cost for systems that paid benefits independent of retirement.

I turn now to a series of simple models. The first is a three-period model, with variation in the additive disutility of labor being the only element of variation in the population. After considering this model with a forward-looking retirement decision, I consider the same model with myopic retirement decisions. First, I explore an assumption that will be made throughout.

---

5. Learning about mortality opens the important issue of the timing of annuitization, an issue considered in Brugiavini (1993) and Sheshinski (1999).

6.2   Moral Hazard Constraint

In a first-best solution, the marginal utility of consumption is the same for a worker whether working or not at any particular time. This will not satisfy the incentive compatibility constraint under the plausible assumption that if marginal utilities were equated, then the level of utility would be higher without work. This condition holds if the only difference between utility functions when working or not is an additive disutility of work. Formally, we state the assumption:

Assume that the moral hazard condition is met: that *if marginal utilities are equated, utility would be higher without work for all values of the additive portion of the disutility of work a*:

$$\text{If } u'[x] = v'[c], \quad \text{then } u[x] < v[c]. \tag{6.3}$$

Note that this is a "normality" assumption. If a worker were just indifferent to work, $u[x] = v[c]$, then small equal increases in consumption whether working or not would make utility lower if working and so result in retirement since $u'[x] < v'[c]$.

With this assumption we have a second-best problem if we have asymmetric information about the disutility of work or the ability to work. That is the interesting case and the one I explore.

6.3   Varying Disutility

Consider a three-period model where everyone works in the first period, no one works in the third period, and work is a choice variable in the second period.[6] Assume

---

6. This assumption can be interpreted in terms of age-varying disutilities of labor—ones that are all low in period 1 and all high in period 3.

that at the optimum there is some, but not complete, second-period work. Assume that individuals do no saving. Assume that the disutility of labor, a, $a \geq 0$, is distributed in the population, with distribution $F[a]$, density $f[a]$.

Denote consumption for workers by the period of consumption $-x_1$ for everyone while working in period 1 and x_2 in period 2 for those working in period 2. Denote consumption for retirees by the length of their work career $-c_1$ in both periods 2 and 3 for those who retired after one period of work, and c_2 in period 3 for those who retired after period 2. We assume constant consumption after retirement. This is optimal in some but not all of the models analyzed.

6.4   Models of Retirement Incentives

6.4.1   Forward-Looking Case

Assume a forward-looking lifetime-utility maximization when making the retirement decision. Then the marginal second-period worker has the same lifetime utility with and without work in the second period. Thus, equating lifetime utilities with and without second-period work, disutility for the marginal worker, denoted a^*, satisfies

$$a^* = u[x_2] + v[c_2] - 2v[c_1]. \tag{6.4}$$

The implicit tax on second-period work is the marginal product plus benefits if not working less the sum of the current net wage and future benefits if working. Thus the implicit tax is

$$T = n - x_2 - c_2 + 2c_1. \tag{6.5}$$

Social welfare integrates lifetime utility over the entire population. The maximization of social welfare has a resource constraint and recognizes the endogeneity of the retirement decision as follows:

$$\text{Maximize}_{x,c} \quad \int_0^{a^*} \{u[x_1] + u[x_2] - 2a + v[c_2]\} \, dF[a]$$

$$+ \int_{a^*}^{\infty} \{u[x_1] - a + 2v[c_1]\} \, dF[a]$$

$$\text{subject to} \quad E + \int_0^{a^*} \{x_1 + x_2 - 2n + c_2\} \, dF[a] \qquad (6.6)$$

$$+ \int_{a^*}^{\infty} \{x_1 - n + 2c_1\} \, dF[a] \leq 0$$

where $\quad a^* = u[x_2] + v[c_2] - 2v[c_1],$

and E represents net government expenditures other than the retirement program. Solving the FOC (which is done in the proof below), we have

$$u'[x_1] = \lambda,$$

$$u'[x_2] = \lambda \Big/ \left\{ 1 + \lambda T \frac{f[a^*]}{F[a^*]} \right\},$$

$$v'[c_1] = \lambda \Big/ \left\{ 1 - \lambda T \frac{f[a^*]}{1 - F[a^*]} \right\}, \qquad (6.7)$$

$$v'[c_2] = \lambda \Big/ \left\{ 1 + \lambda T \frac{f[a^*]}{F[a^*]} \right\}.$$

The FOCs reflect the direct marginal utility gain and resource cost of increasing any consumption level, which affects either $F[a^*]$ or $1 - F[a^*]$ of the population. In addition, there is an indirect effect coming from the induced change in labor supply, reflected in the change in a^* and the number of marginal workers, $f[a^*]$. By the envelope theorem, there is no first-order change in utility for someone at the margin choosing to work. There is a first-order impact on resource use, equal to the implicit tax on work. From the FOC, the moral hazard constraint and the assumption that the optimum has an interior solution— some but not complete work in period 2—we have

THEOREM. Assuming the moral hazard constraint and that the optimum is internal (some work and some retirement in period 2), at the optimum, there is positive taxation of second-period work:

$$T = n - x_2 - c_2 + 2c_1 > 0. \tag{6.8}$$

And we have

$$v'[c_2] = u'[x_2] < u'[x_1] < v'[c_1], \tag{6.9}$$

implying

$$c_2 > c_1, x_2 > x_1. \tag{6.10}$$

COROLLARY. If u and v differ by an additive constant, then

$$c_2 = x_2 > x_1 > c_1. \tag{6.11}$$

Proof. The solution to the FOCs above can by seen by solving the FOCs, which are

$$u'[x_1] = \lambda$$

$$u'[x_2] = \lambda - \lambda\{n - x_2 - c_2 + 2c_1\} \frac{f[a^*]}{F[a^*]} \frac{da^*}{dx_2}$$

$$= \lambda - \lambda T \frac{f[a^*]}{F[a^*]} u'[x_2]$$

$$v'[c_1] = \lambda - \lambda\{n - x_2 - c_2 + 2c_1\}\frac{f[a^*]}{1 - F[a^*]}\frac{da^*}{dc_1}\bigg/2$$

$$= \lambda + \lambda T \frac{f[a^*]}{1 - F[a^*]} v'[c_1]$$

$$v'[c_2] = \lambda - \lambda\{n - x_2 - c_2 + 2c_1\}\frac{f[a^*]}{F[a^*]}\frac{da^*}{dc_2}$$

$$= \lambda - \lambda T \frac{f[a^*]}{F[a^*]} v'[c_2]. \tag{6.12}$$

Examining the FOCs, we have $u'[x_2] = v'[c_2]$, implying that if u and v differ by an additive constant, then $x_2 = c_2$. Moreover, we have

LEMMA 1.   If and only if $T = n - x_2 - c_2 + 2c_1 > 0$, then $x_2 > x_1$, $c_2 > c_1$, and $u'[x_1] < v'[c_1]$.

Proof of Lemma 1.   From the FOCs, the sign of T determines the difference between the ratio of marginal utilities and one.

$$\frac{u'[x_2]}{u'[x_1]} - 1 = \frac{1}{1 + \lambda T \dfrac{f[a^*]}{F[a^*]}} - 1. \tag{6.13}$$

$$\frac{v'[c_2]}{v'[c_1]} - 1 = \frac{1 - \lambda T \dfrac{f[a^*]}{F[a^*]}}{1 + \lambda T \dfrac{f[a^*]}{1 - F[a^*]}} - 1. \tag{6.14}$$

$$\frac{v'[c_1]}{u'[x_1]} = \frac{1}{1 - \lambda T \dfrac{f[a^*]}{1 - F[a^*]}} - 1 \tag{6.15}$$

Proof of Theorem. If $T < 0$, then a^* is zero from the Lemma and the moral hazard constraint. This violates the assumption of an interior solution. ∎

Thus, we have implicit taxation of work in the second period. Moreover second-period work results in higher consumption than first-period work and retirement benefits in period 3 are larger if there was work in period 2. If we have additive disutility, then the replacement rate rises with the age of retirement $(c_1/x_1 < 1 = c_2/x_2)$. The equality of the marginal utilities of c_2 and x_2 reflects the fact that they have the same impact on labor supply given the assumption of a rational forward-looking retirement decision. If we had not set both the utility discount rate and the productivity of capital equal to zero, the marginal utilities would reflect the difference between them.

6.4.2 Forward-Looking Case with Consumption Constraint

If we interpret the model in terms of a payroll tax and retirement benefits, then we implicitly have an age-varying payroll tax in section 6.4.1. It is straightforward to extend the analysis to a constant payroll tax. With constant earnings levels, this implies that consumption of workers must be the same in both periods:

$$x_1 = x_2 = x. \tag{6.16}$$

Having an additional constraint, the optimum is not as good as above since the constraint would be violated in the optimum without the constraint. From the FOC, the moral hazard constraint, and the assumption of an interior optimum we have the following theorem (which is proven in the appendix).

THEOREM. Assuming the moral hazard constraint and that the optimum is internal (some work and some retirement in period 2), at the optimum there is positive taxation of second-period work:

$$T = n - x - c_2 + 2c_1 > 0, \qquad (6.17)$$

and we have

$$v'[c_2] < u'[x] < v'[c_1], \qquad (6.18)$$

implying

$$c_2 > c_1. \qquad (6.19)$$

COROLLARY. If u and v differ by an additive constant, then

$$c_2 > x > c_1. \qquad (6.20)$$

6.4.3 Myopic Model

The preceding models assumed a forward-looking retirement decision, so that individual choice matched the social welfare evaluation. We now assume that everyone is shortsighted and the marginal second-period worker considers only the utility in the second period when making the retirement decision. Thus the marginal worker has disutility that satisfies

$$a^* = u[x_2] - v[c_1]. \qquad (6.21)$$

The assumption of an interior optimum now requires different underlying conditions than does the same assumption in the forward-looking case.

For the resource constraint, the implicit tax on work is the same as in (6.5):

$$T = n - x_2 - c_2 + 2c_1. \tag{6.22}$$

Define the *apparent tax* for a myopic worker as the wage plus current benefit less current consumption if working:

$$A = n - x_2 + c_1. \tag{6.23}$$

This is the resource impact of the part of the implicit tax that affects the retirement decision.

Social welfare maximization is now as follows:

$$\text{Maximize}_{x,c} \int_0^{a^*} \{u[x_1] + u[x_2] - 2a + v[c_2]\} \, dF[a]$$

$$+ \int_{a^*}^{\infty} \{u[x_1] - a + 2v[c_1]\} \, dF[a]$$

$$\text{subject to} \quad E + \int_0^{a^*} \{x_1 + x_2 - 2n + c_2\} \, dF[a] \tag{6.24}$$

$$+ \int_{a^*}^{\infty} \{x_1 - n + 2c_1\} \, dF[a] \leq 0$$

where $\quad a^* = u[x_2] - v[c_1]$.

Solving the FOCs produces

$$u'[x_1] = v'[c_2] = \lambda,$$

$$u'[x_2] = \lambda \bigg/ \left\{ 1 + (v[c_2] - v[c_1] + \lambda T) \frac{f[a^*]}{F[a^*]} \right\}, \tag{6.25}$$

$$v'[c_1] = \lambda \bigg/ \left\{ 1 - (v[c_2] - v[c_1] + \lambda T) \frac{f[a^*]}{1 - F[a^*]} \bigg/ 2 \right\}.$$

Note that the critical term in the FOCs is $(v[c_2] - v[c_1] + \lambda T)$, where it was just (λT) above. This change reflects the error (relative to the social welfare function evaluation) in private retirement decisions of ignoring the impact of the second-period work decision on third-period benefits. That is, a change in labor supply affects the social welfare function directly as well as changing the cost of the program. Thus the optimal tax has a Pigouvian flavor as well as a redistributive component—the tax is also trying to correct for the deviation between social and private evaluations.

THEOREM.   Assuming the moral hazard constraint and that the optimum is internal (some work and some retirement in period 2), at the optimum we have

$$v[c_2] - v[c_1] + \lambda T > 0, \tag{6.26}$$

and we have

$$u'[x_2] < u'[x_1] = v'[c_2] < v'[c_1], \tag{6.27}$$

implying

$$c_2 > c_1, x_2 > x_1. \tag{6.28}$$

COROLLARY.   If u and v differ by an additive constant, then

$$x_2 > x_1 = c_2 > c_1. \tag{6.29}$$

Proof.   We obtain the conditions above by solving the FOC:

$$u'[x_1] = \lambda,$$

$$u'[x_2] + \{v[c_2] - v[c_1]\} \frac{f[a^*]}{F[a^*]} u'[x_2] = \lambda - \lambda\{n - x_2 - c_2 + 2c_1\}$$

$$\times \frac{f[a^*]}{F[a^*]} u'[x_2]$$

$$= \lambda - \lambda T \frac{f[a^*]}{F[a^*]} u'[x_2],$$

$$v'[c_1] - \{v[c_2] - v[c_1]\} \frac{f[a^*]}{F[a^*]} v'[c_1]/2 = \lambda + \lambda\{n - x_2 - c_2 + 2c_1\}$$

$$\times \frac{f[a^*]}{1 - F[a^*]} v'[c_1]/2$$

$$= \lambda + \lambda T \frac{f[a^*]}{1 - F[a^*]} v'[c_1]/2,$$

$$v'[c_2] = \lambda. \tag{6.30}$$

At the optimum, $v'[c_2] = u'[x_1]$. Since there is some work, $u[x_2] > v[c_1]$. The moral hazard constraint then implies $u'[x_2] < v'[c_1]$. Paralleling the proof above, with an interior solution, this implies that $(v[c_2] - v[c_1] + \lambda T) > 0$ and the remaining condition follows from the FOC. ∎

Since neither x_1 nor c_2 affects labor supply, the marginal utilities of these consumption levels are equated. In contrast, changes in the other two consumption levels do affect labor supply, and in opposite directions. For the case of an additive disutility of work, with a forward-looking retirement decision, we have equation (6.11):

$$c_2 = x_2 > x_1 > c_1.$$

In contrast, with a myopic retirement decision, we have (6.29):

$$x_2 > x_1 = c_2 > c_1.$$

The relative sizes of x_2, x_1, and c_1 are the same in the two cases, although their magnitudes differ since the FOC are different. However, the relative size of c_2 is different, depending on whether it does or does not affect retirement.

It appears that the tax on work may be positive or negative since there is a need to subsidize work to offset myopia. The apparent tax is larger than the tax, akin to a corrective Pigouvian subsidy to offset the failure of the second-period work decision to reflect third-period benefits. This tends to offset the incentive arguments discussed earlier.

$$
\begin{aligned}
\lambda A &= \lambda(n - x_2 + c_1) \\
&= \lambda\{n - x_2 - c_2 + 2c_1\} + \lambda(c_2 - c_1) \\
&= \lambda T + \lambda(c_2 - c_1) \\
&> \lambda T.
\end{aligned}
\tag{6.31}
$$

With worker myopia, we want to adjust for the difference between the perceived incentive and the actual utility payoff by raising consumption if working and by lowering the benefit if taking early retirement. This tends to offset the optimal tax considerations analyzed earlier, that we want to tax those with low disutility of labor by taxing long careers.

6.5   Extension

If benefits could be different in the two retirement periods for a worker retiring after one period of work, the optimum would have higher benefits in period 3 than in period 2.

6.6   Stochastic Earnings

In the three previous models, there was ex ante heterogeneity, without individual uncertainty. I turn now to one important issue of individual uncertainty—uncertainty as to length of career. Some careers are cut short because of measurable disability. A disability insurance program is a valuable social insurance program, even though disability will only be measured with both type I and type II errors. Unemployment insurance can also help with the transition to retirement for some workers. Again, there will be errors in measuring true unemployment. Some careers will be sensibly cut short without being covered by such programs. In part this can happen because of errors in measurement, because work has become too taxing, (even though there is no measurable disability), and because the employment opportunities that are available are not worth pursuing. For dealing with such uncertainties, socially provided insurance against a short career can add to expected lifetime utilities. To explore this issue, Mirrlees and I have written four papers, examining models where all workers are ex ante identical (Diamond and Mirrlees 1978, 1986, 2000, forthcoming). Here, I consider them briefly.

Continue with the basic three-period model employed above. Assume that everyone works in period 1 and no one works in period 3 and there are no savings. Stochastically, some people can work in period 2 and some cannot. If there are no savings opportunities, then this is equivalent to a heterogeneous agent model, although one with discrete types instead of a continuum of types. However, once we extend the model to incorporate more periods of possible inability to work, then the two models become different. Given asymmetry of information as to who can work in period 2, we have a moral hazard problem. Given the moral hazard constraint and the presence of just two types, the compensation for early retirees should be as large as possible without resulting in retirement of those able to work. The homogeneity of those able to work converts this problem into one of just inducing labor supply. Even with this difference, we get the same results as above—there should be some taxation of work and the return to work should show up in both a rising wage and a rising benefit for later retirement. Extending the model to more periods preserves these results and provides a further result—that the implicit tax on work should decrease with age, reaching zero at an age where everyone still able to work chooses to retire (Diamond and Mirrlees 1978).

This further result can be seen intuitively since higher later wages serve as an incentive to work at all earlier ages. So there is more of an incentive effect for a later wage than an earlier one. However, this result depends critically on the assumption of an ex ante homogeneous population. Otherwise, the shape of the distribution of ex ante differences (e.g., in disutility) would also affect the time shape of optimal implicit taxation. We see that in the previous FOCs that include a hazard, $(f[a^*])/(1 - F[a^*])$.

These results extend to two additional models—one where the wage must be constant (e.g., payroll tax financed, Diamond and Mirrlees 1986) and one where individuals can save without the government being able to observe savings (Diamond and Mirrlees, forthcoming). The latter is interesting since it involves individuals saving in order to weaken the government's ability to discourage early retirement. That is, someone considering an earlier retirement would save more to finance an earlier retirement. Thus the government would like to discourage savings in order to do a better job of providing insurance. We have also explored the results with more general preferences (Diamond and Mirrlees 2000).

Appendix: Varying Disutility: Forward-Looking Case with Consumption Constraint

We assume that consumption of workers must be the same in both periods:

$$x_1 = x_2 = x. \tag{6A.1}$$

The implicit tax on second-period work is

$$T = n - x - c_2 + 2c_1. \tag{6A.2}$$

The optimization is as follows:

$$\text{Maximize}_{x,c} \quad \int_0^{a^*} \{2u[x] - 2a + v[c_2]\}\, dF[a]$$

$$+ \int_{a^*}^{\infty} \{u[x] - a + 2v[c_1]\}\, dF[a]$$

$$\text{subject to} \quad E + \int_0^{a^*} \{2x - 2n + c_2\}\, dF[a] \tag{6A.3}$$

$$+ \int_{a^*}^{\infty} \{x - n + 2c_1\}\, dF[a] \le 0$$

where $\quad a^* = u[x] + v[c_2] - 2v[c_1].$

FOC:

$$u'[x] = \lambda - \lambda\{n - x - c_2 + 2c_1\} \frac{f[a^*]}{1 + F[a^*]} \frac{da^*}{dx}$$

$$= \lambda - \lambda T \frac{f[a^*]}{1 + F[a^*]} u'[x],$$

$$v'[c_1] = \lambda - \lambda\{n - x - c_2 + 2c_1\} \frac{f[a^*]}{1 - F[a^*]} \frac{da^*}{dc_1} \bigg/ 2$$

$$= \lambda + \lambda T \frac{f[a^*]}{1 - F[a^*]} v'[c_1],$$

$$v'[c_2] = \lambda - \lambda\{n - x - c_2 + 2c_1\}\frac{f[a^*]}{F[a^*]}\frac{da^*}{dc_2}$$

$$= \lambda - \lambda T \frac{f[a^*]}{F[a^*]} v'[c_2]. \tag{6A.4}$$

Solving, we have

$$u'[x] = \lambda \Big/ \left\{ 1 + \lambda T \frac{f[a^*]}{1 + F[a^*]} \right\}$$

$$v'[c_1] = \lambda \Big/ \left\{ 1 - \lambda T \frac{f[a^*]}{1 - F[a^*]} \right\} \tag{6A.5}$$

$$v'[c_2] = \lambda \Big/ \left\{ 1 + \lambda T \frac{f[a^*]}{F[a^*]} \right\}$$

Examining the FOC, we have

LEMMA 1.   If and only if $T = n - x - c_2 + 2c_1 > 0$, then $c_2 > c_1$, $v'[c_2] < u'[x] < v'[c_1]$.

Proof.

$$\frac{v'[c_2]}{v'[c_1]} - 1 = \frac{1 - \lambda T \dfrac{f[a^*]}{1 - F[a^*]}}{1 + \lambda T \dfrac{f[a^*]}{F[a^*]}} - 1. \tag{6A.6}$$

$$\frac{u'[x]}{v'[c_1]} - 1 = \frac{1 - \lambda T \dfrac{f[a^*]}{1 - F[a^*]}}{1 + \lambda T \dfrac{f[a^*]}{1 + F[a^*]}} - 1. \tag{6A.7}$$

$$\frac{u'[x]}{v'[c_2]} - 1 = \frac{1 + \lambda T \dfrac{f[a^*]}{F[a^*]}}{1 + \lambda T \dfrac{f[a^*]}{1 + F[a^*]}} - 1. \tag{6A.8}$$

THEOREM.   At the optimum there is positive taxation of
second-period work:

$$T = n - x - c_2 + 2c_1 > 0,$$ (6A.9)

and we have

$$v'[c_2] < u'[x] < v'[c_1],$$ (6A.10)

$$c_2 > c_1.$$ (6A.11)

Proof.   If $T < 0$, then a^* is zero from the lemma and the
moral hazard constraint contradicting the assumption of
an interior optimum.   ∎

7

Models of Optimal Retirement Incentives with Varying Life Expectancy

Workers vary in their life expectancies. Therefore, any increase in annuitized benefits for working beyond the earliest eligibility age will impact differentially across workers. If an adjustment is actuarially fair on average, it is an implicit tax on some workers and an implicit subsidy for others. This chapter continues analysis of retirement incentives, while continuing to ignore differences in earnings levels. Chapter 6 contained a contrast between optimal systems when workers are fully forward-looking and when they are myopic. This chapter contains a contrast between optimal systems with and without individual savings after retirement. Two models are considered—with no savings (as in chapter 6), and with savings starting in period 2 (but not in period 1) that are invested in perfect (individually actuarially fair) annuities. Further contrasts in outcomes relative to market structure could be done by examining additional models—with savings that are invested in bonds (with an allocation of estates, perhaps through 100 percent estate taxation) and with savings that are invested in group annuities (actuarially fair for the group).

It remains the case that for reasons of income distribution and insurance, in both models analyzed there should be some taxation of work for the marginal worker eligible for retirement benefits. The return to work shows up in both higher net earnings when working and higher later benefits for those who delay retirement in the model without savings. However, this may not be the case in the model with perfect private annuities where retirees may receive only a lump sum—no annuities.[1] The portion of the work incentive coming in the form of larger annuitized retirement benefits for late retirees would overpay the nonmarginal retirees, who have longer life expectancy. That is, by using the private market, which prices annuities differently for those with different life expectancies, the government could induce the same labor supply while paying the nonmarginal late retirees less. Thus, as we will see, the optimum may provide benefits to late retirees only as a lump sum. Since using only a lump sum may leave those with the longest expected life with low consumption, the optimum may use both a lump sum and annuitized benefits.

Similarly, the use of the private annuity market can allow increased consumption for nonmarginal early retirees without affecting labor supply. The government cannot make early retirement benefits as large as it would like because of the disincentive to work. Thus early retirees can have high social marginal utilities of consumption. But those with very short life expectancies are not marginal workers. By allowing them to substitute market

---

1. In a continuous-time model, there are three sources of compensation: net wages while working, a lump sum at retirement, and annuitized benefits after retirement. In this discrete-time model, the first two are lumped together.

annuities for the government annuity, we distribute more
to those with short lives. Use of a lump sum alone can be
optimal. It might not be the case that the entire lifetime
benefit is paid as a lump sum, since that might leave some
with very short life expectancies with sufficiently high
consumption that they have low social marginal utilities
of consumption.

It is worth remembering that these results occur in
models with fully forward-looking retirement and post-
retirement savings decisions and full annuitization. Moreover, in these models all early retirees are less well-off;
there are no differences in private wealth on reaching the
early retirement age that would result in some early retirees having high consumption and so low marginal utility of consumption.

The models are a four-period version of the model in
chapter 6 with a fully rational forward-looking retirement
decision. Everyone survives through period 3, with some
retirees dying between periods 3 and 4. It is assumed that
everyone knows his or her survival probabilities and that
all workers have the same earnings potential. Also, the
models contrast economies with different worker savings
and investing behavior, but with everyone showing the
same behavior within a model. It would be interesting to
consider models with mixes of types (as in Feldstein
1985).

7.1   Moral Hazard Constraint

As in the previous chapter, we use two different utility
functions when working and not: $u[x] - a$, a function of
consumption when working, x, and $v[c]$, a function of
consumption when retired, c. We assume both utility

functions are concave. We continue to make the plausible assumption that if marginal utilities were equated, then the level of utility would be higher without work. This is the case if the only difference between utility functions is an additive disutility of work. More generally, we state the assumption:

Assume that the moral hazard condition is met: that if marginal utilities are equated, utility would be higher without work for all values of a:

If $u'[x] = v'[c]$,   then $u[x] < v[c]$.   (7.1)

Note that this is a "normality" assumption. If a worker were just indifferent to work, $u[x] = v[c]$, then small equal increases in consumption whether working or not would raise utility in the two states by $u'[x]$ and $v'[c]$. Since $u'[x] < v'[c]$, this would give lower utility if working and so result in retirement.

With this assumption we have a second-best problem if we have asymmetric information about life expectancy. That is the interesting case and the one I explore. To ignore zero corners, we also assume that the marginal utility of consumption would be infinite at zero consumption, whether working or not.

7.2   Model with Varying Life Span and Disutility: No Savings

We use a four-period model where everyone works in the first period, no one works in the third or fourth periods, and some people do work and some do not in the second period. As previously, assume that at the optimum there is an interior solution—some, but not complete, second-period work. Assume that real social security benefits vary with age at retirement but not age at receipt.[2]

Everyone survives to period 3, but only some survive to period 4. Let p be the probability of worker p surviving to period 4. Let a_p ($a_p \geq 0$) be the additive portion of the disutility of labor in periods 1 and 2 for someone who has the probability p of surviving to period 4.[3] We assume that a_p is nonincreasing in p, that is, $da_p/dp \leq 0$. That is, those with longer lives are more capable of working in period 2, as measured by disutility. Assume p can vary between p_0 and p_1, and has distribution $F[p]$ and density $f[p]$.

We assume additive preferences and zero utility discount and interest rates. We continue the same notation as above—subscripts on consumption when working refer to the period, while those on consumption when retired refer to the period of retirement. A worker chooses between two plans. With no work in period 2, expected lifetime utility for worker p is $u[x_1] - a_p + (2+p)v[c_1]$. With work in period 2, expected lifetime utility for worker p is $u[x_1] + u[x_2] - 2a_p + (1+p)v[c_2]$.

By assumption there is an interior solution—some people retire early and some retire late. Thus there is a marginal worker. With a forward-looking retirement decision, the marginal second-period worker has survival probability p^* and disutility that equates lifetime utility with the two plans and so satisfies

$$a_{p^*} = u[x_2] + (1+p^*)v[c_2] - (2+p^*)v[c_1]. \tag{7.2}$$

---

2. It would be interesting to examine a time-varying annuity.
3. We could have considered two dimensions of variation in the population—disutility and life expectancy—and made an assumption on their covariation in the population. Instead, we have continued to assume a single dimension of variation with a fixed relationship between disutility and life expectancy.

Differentiating implicitly, we have

$$\frac{dp^*}{dx_2} = -u'[x_2]/D,$$

$$\frac{dp^*}{dc_1} = (2+p^*)v'[c_1]/D, \tag{7.3}$$

$$\frac{dp^*}{dc_2} = -(1+p^*)v'[c_2]/D,$$

where $D = v[c_2] - v[c_1] - da_p/dp$. There is a unique solution to the marginal condition (7.2) provided that $c_2 \geq c_1$. Moreover, with this condition, we have $D > 0$. We will show that the optimum has this property.

The implicit tax on work measures the impact on the government budget of additional work. The implicit tax on second-period work for worker p is the marginal product plus expected future benefits if not working less the sum of current consumption and expected future benefits if working. Thus the implicit tax for worker p is

$$T[p] = n - x_2 - (1+p)c_2 + (2+p)c_1. \tag{7.4}$$

With $c_2 > c_1$, implicit taxes are less for those with longer life expectancies and larger for those with shorter life expectancies.

Social welfare maximization, assuming simple addition of lifetime utilities, is now as follows:

$$\text{Maximize}_{x,c} \quad \int_{p_0}^{p^*} \{u[x_1] - a_p + (2+p)v[c_1]\} \, dF[p]$$

$$+ \int_{p^*}^{p_1} \{u[x_1] + u[x_2] - 2a_p + (1+p)v[c_2]\} \, dF[p]$$

subject to
$$E + \int_{p_0}^{p^*} \{x_1 - n + (2+p)c_1\}\, dF[p]$$

$$+ \int_{p^*}^{p_1} \{x_1 + x_2 - 2n + (1+p)c_2\}\, dF[p] \le 0$$

where p^* satisfies $\quad a_{p^*} = u[x_2] + (1+p^*)v[c_2] - (2+p^*)v[c_1].$
$$(7.5)$$

Deriving the FOC and rearranging terms, as shown in the proof, the FOC can be written as

$$u'[x_1] = \lambda,$$

$$u'[x_2] = \lambda \Big/ \left\{ 1 + \lambda \frac{T[p^*]}{D} \frac{f[p^*]}{1 - F[p^*]} \right\},$$

$$v'[c_1] = \lambda \Big/ \left\{ 1 - \lambda \frac{T[p^*]}{D} \frac{f[p^*]}{F[p^*]} \frac{2 + p^*}{2 + P_0[p^*]} \right\},$$

$$v'[c_2] = \lambda \Big/ \left\{ 1 + \lambda \frac{T[p^*]}{D} \frac{f[p^*]}{1 - F[p^*]} \frac{1 + p^*}{1 + P_1[p^*]} \right\},$$

$$(7.6)$$

where $P_0[p]$ and $P_1[p]$ are the average survival probabilities for those below and above p:

$$P_0[p] = \int_{p_0}^{p} s\, dF[s] / F[p],$$

$$P_1[p] = \int_{p}^{p_1} s\, dF[s] / (1 - F[p]).$$
$$(7.7)$$

Thus we have

$$P_0[p] < p < P_1[p].$$
$$(7.8)$$

Naturally the FOC distinguish the average life expectancies of the early and late retirees.

Examining the FOC, the Lagrangian equals the marginal utility of consumption in period 1 since there are no incentive effects associated with this net wage. Each of the other three consumption levels have an effect on retirement decisions, and so on the resource constraint. Increasing the net wage in period 2 or the level of benefits for late retirees encourages more work and so improves the resource constraint given a positive implicit tax on work. Increasing the benefit for early retirees has the opposite effect. Naturally these incentives affect the optimal levels of consumption. The qualitative results are summarized in

THEOREM.   At the optimum we have $T[p^*] > 0, D > 0$,

$$u'[x_2] < v'[c_2] < u'[x_1] < v'[c_1] \qquad (7.9)$$

implying

$$c_2 > c_1, x_2 > x_1. \qquad (7.10)$$

COROLLARY.   If u and v differ by an additive constant, then

$$x_2 > c_2 > x_1 > c_1. \qquad (7.11)$$

Proof. The FOCs as stated above come from solving the FOC:

$$u'[x_1] = \lambda,$$

$$(u'[x_2] - \lambda)(1 - F[p^*]) = \lambda T[p^*] f[p^*] \frac{dp^*}{dx_2}$$

$$= -\lambda \frac{T[p^*]}{D} f[p^*] u'[x_2],$$

$$(v'[c_1] - \lambda)(2 + P_0[p^*])F[p^*] = \lambda T[p^*]f[p^*]\frac{dp^*}{dc_1}$$

$$= \lambda\frac{T[p^*]}{D}f[p^*](2 + p^*)v'[c_1],$$

$$(v'[c_2] - \lambda)(1 + P_1[p^*])(1 - F[p^*]) = \lambda T[p^*]f[p^*]\frac{dp^*}{dc_2}$$

$$= -\lambda\frac{T[p^*]}{D}f[p^*](1 + p^*)v'[c_2].$$

$$(7.12)$$

LEMMA 1. If and only if $T[p^*]/D > 0$, then $u'[x_2] < v'[c_2]$, $v'[c_2] < u'[x_1] < v'[c_1]$.

Proof of Lemma 1.

$$\frac{u'[x_2]}{v'[c_2]} = \frac{K + (1 + p^*)/(1 + P_1[p^*])}{K + 1} < 1, \qquad (7.13)$$

where $K^{-1} = \lambda(T[p^*]/D)(f[p^*])/(1 - F[p^*])$.

The first inequality follows from the sign of $K > 0$ and $(1 + p^*)/(1 + P_1[p^*]) < 1$. The rest follow from the FOC.

LEMMA 2. If $T[p^*]/D > 0$, then $T[p^*] > 0$, $D > 0$.

Proof of Lemma 2. If $D < 0$, then $v[c_2] < v[c_1]$ since $da_p/dp < 0$. From Lemma 1, $v'[c_2] < v'[c_1]$. This is a contradiction.

PROOF OF THEOREM. If $T[p^*]/D > 0$, the results follow from the lemmas. If $T[p^*]/D \leq 0$, then we contradict the assumption that $a_{p^*} > 0$ with the following argument. If $T[p^*]$ is zero, then all marginal utilities are equal and from the moral hazard constraint we have a contradiction. With $T[p^*] < 0$, lemma 1 gives the same contradiction. A similar argument works with $T[p^*] > 0$ and $D < 0$. ∎

Contrasting this optimum with the case with uniform life expectancies, we see that some workers are taxed and some may be subsidized at the optimum. The levels of consumption provided depend on the life expectancies of the different groups receiving different benefits. The relationship among probabilities, $P_0[p] < p < P_1[p]$, gives us the size of the terms in the FOC, (7.6), that would equal one if life expectancies were all the same: $(2 + p^*)/(2 + P_0[p^*]) > 1$ and $(1 + p^*)/(1 + P_1[p^*]) < 1$. Thus the variance in life expectancy would matter for the optimum, with mean held constant. Just accounting for these terms (and ignoring the impact of a change in the distribution of life expectancies on other terms in the FOC), more variance in life expectancies tends to lower both c_1 and c_2. As noted at the start of this chapter, the wage for working in period 2 is larger than the wage in period 1 and delaying retirement increases the retirement benefit in periods 3 and 4.

7.3   Discrete-Types Model

In order to understand better the workings of this model (and to have a base for the model with savings that follows), we now explore a very artificial model. We start with the model of chapter 6 where workers vary in the additive disutility of labor but not life expectancy. We refer to these workers as type-B workers and denote the (independent) probability of each of them surviving to period 4 by p_B. Denote the distribution of additive disutilities of type-B workers by $F[a]$. To this model, we add two additional types of workers, with survival probabilities satisfying $p_A < p_B < p_C$. We assume that the additive disutility of labor does not vary within each of these

two other types. We assume that the optimum occurs with some type-B workers retiring early and some retiring late. Then, the optimum has the character (as in chapter 6) that there is an implicit tax on work for the type-B workers, that early retirees have higher marginal utility of consumption after period 1 than the marginal utility in period 1, and that late retirees have lower marginal utility of consumption after period 1 than in period 1 (as a consequence of the moral hazard assumption). This implies that the government would like to increase consumption of early retirees. The presence of small numbers of types A and C do not change this. With only type-B workers there would be no distortion of the savings decision. Adding the other two types of workers changes this result.

Denote the fraction of type-B workers who retire early by β. If the marginal retiree is denoted by a^*, then we can write β in terms of a^*: $\beta[a^*] = 1 - F[a^*]$. With the same assumptions as above, those with shorter life expectancy will also retire early, while those with longer life expectancy will also retire late. We denote the relative numbers of the three types by f_A, 1, and f_C. The social welfare maximization is as follows:

$$\text{Maximize}_{x,c} \quad f_A(u[x_1] - a_A + (2 + p_A)v[c_1])$$

$$+ \beta[a^*](u[x_1] + (2 + p_B)v[c_1]) - \int_{a^*}^{\infty} a\,dF[a]$$

$$+ (1 - \beta[a^*])(u[x_1] + u[x_2] + (1 + p_B)v[c_2])$$

$$- 2\int_{0}^{a^*} a\,dF[a]$$

$$+ f_C(u[x_1] + u[x_2] - 2a_C + (1 + p_C)v[c_2])$$

subject to $E + (f_A + 1 + f_C)(x_1 - n) + (f_A(2 + p_A)$

$$+ \beta(2 + p_B))c_1 + (1 - \beta + f_C)(x_2 - n)$$

$$+ ((1 - \beta)(1 + p_B) + f_C(1 + p_C))c_2 \leq 0,$$

$$x_1 \geq 0; \ c_1 \geq 0; \ x_2 \geq 0; \ c_2 \geq 0,$$

with a^* given by $(2 + p_B)v[c_1] = u[x_2] - a^* + (1 + p_B)v[c_2]$.

$$(7.14)$$

With the marginal type-B worker indifferent to working, the only effect of changing β is the impact on the resource constraint: $-T[p_B]d\beta$, where $T[p_B]$ is the implicit tax on work. Since all of the type-A workers retire early and all the type-C workers retire late, these types appear in different FOCs for payment levels. As before, there is no incentive effect associated with first-period consumption:

$$u'[x_1] - \lambda = 0. \tag{7.15}$$

In considering the other consumption levels, we need to include the impact on β

$$(f_A(2 + p_A) + \beta(2 + p_B))(v'[c_1] - \lambda)$$

$$= -\lambda T[p_B]\frac{d\beta}{dc_1}$$

$$= -\lambda T[p_B]\frac{d\beta}{da^*}\frac{da^*}{dc_1}$$

$$= \lambda T[p_B]f[a^*](2 + p_B)v'[c_1]$$

$$\equiv \mu(2 + p_B)v'[c_1], \tag{7.16}$$

where we have introduced μ, which is positive by similar arguments to those earlier. Similarly, for the benefits to late retirees, we have

$$(1 - \beta + f_C)(u'[x_2] - \lambda) = -\mu u'[x_2] \tag{7.17}$$

$$((1 - \beta)(1 + p_B) + f_C(1 + p_C))(v'[c_2] - \lambda)$$
$$= -\mu(1 + p_B)v'[c_2]. \tag{7.18}$$

Rearranging terms, we have

$$u'[x_1] = \lambda \tag{7.19}$$

$$\left(f_A \frac{(2 + p_A)}{(2 + p_B)} + \beta - \mu \right) v'[c_1] = \left(f_A \frac{(2 + p_A)}{(2 + p_B)} + \beta \right) \lambda \tag{7.20}$$

$$(1 - \beta + f_C + \mu)u'[x_2] = (1 - \beta + f_C)\lambda \tag{7.21}$$

$$\left(1 - \beta + f_C \frac{(1 + p_C)}{(1 + p_B)} + \mu \right) v'[c_2] = \left(1 - \beta + f_C \frac{(1 + p_C)}{(1 + p_B)} \right) \lambda. \tag{7.22}$$

From the FOC, $\mu > 0$, and

$$v'[c_1] > u'[x_1] = \lambda > v'[c_2] > u'[x_2]. \tag{7.23}$$

First, we note that the presence of type-C workers breaks the equality of marginal utility of consumption across periods for late retirees. With $\mu > 0$ and $(1 + p_C)/(1 + p_B) > 1$, we have a distortion in the savings being done for late retirees, with $u'[x_2]/v'[c_2] < 1$. That is, the late retirees would like to save in the second period if they could. This fact will make the analysis with savings different. The underlying logic is that type-C workers have low social marginal utilities and are paid more than would be necessary to induce them to work. Thus a small distortion in their savings (and those of late retiring type-B workers) necessarily gains more from redistribution (since nonmarginal type-C workers are more likely to

receive benefits in period 4) than it loses from the inefficiency in their savings. This is an example of the logic
presented in chapter 2 behind the result that generically
some distorting taxes are welfare improving.

We would have a similar result for early retirees if we
allowed different benefit levels in period 4 relative to
earlier periods. Denoting benefits in period 4 by c_1', instead of (7.16), the FOCs for c_1 and c_1' become

$$2(f_A + \beta)(v'[c_1] - \lambda) = \mu 2 v'[c_1] \tag{7.24}$$

$$(f_A p_A + \beta p_B)(v'[c_1'] - \lambda) = \mu p_B v'[c_1']. \tag{7.25}$$

Solving, we have

$$(f_A + \beta - \mu)v'[c_1] = (f_A + \beta)\lambda \tag{7.26}$$

$$\left(f_A \frac{p_A}{p_B} + \beta - \mu\right)v'[c_1'] = \left(f_A \frac{p_A}{p_B} + \beta\right)\lambda. \tag{7.27}$$

This confirms the advantage of distorting savings to take
advantage of the fact that some early retirees are not
marginal retirees and can be compensated more. Early
retirees would like to dissave at this optimum:

$$\frac{v'[c_1]}{v'[c_1']} = \frac{(f_A + \beta)\left(f_A \dfrac{p_A}{p_B} + \beta - \mu\right)}{\left(f_A \dfrac{p_A}{p_B} + \beta\right)(f_A + \beta - \mu)} < 1. \tag{7.28}$$

We turn next to a model with savings, which introduces
the option of paying benefits fully or partially as a lump
sum. As we will see, this is irrelevant when there is only
one type of worker but becomes relevant with more than
one type.

7.4   Model with Varying Life Span and Disutility: With Savings Invested in Perfect Annuities

In the model just analyzed, the government directly controls consumption, but subject to restrictions from asymmetric information. If there is the possibility of private savings, then the government would have less control, although it might be able to exploit the differences in the different workers' propensities to save and the differences between the assets in which they save and the form of government benefits. We turn now to a model with private savings, with savings invested in perfect annuities. With perfect annuities, we are assuming that the market can distinguish life expectancies, but the government cannot or chooses not to. A central question is whether the government wants to make use of this ability of the market. As we will see, the answer is yes. The government wants to encourage work at the margin. But the portion of the encouragement coming in the form of larger annuitized benefits for late retirees overpays the nonmarginal retirees, who have longer life expectancy. That is, by making some use of the private market, which prices annuities differently for those with different life expectancies, the government could induce the same labor supply while paying the nonmarginal late retirees less.

Similarly, the government cannot make early retirement benefits as large as it would like because of the disincentive to work. But those with very short life expectancy are not marginal workers. By allowing them to substitute market annuities for some of the government annuity, we distribute more to those with short lives. It might not be the case that the entire lifetime benefit is paid as a lump sum, since that might leave some with very short (long) life expectancies with sufficiently high (low) consumption that they have low (high) social marginal utilities of consumption. These results depend critically on the rationality of savings among retirees and on the full use of private annuitization, something we do not observe.

As earlier, we assume a small number of different types of workers. We assume that the optimum calls for some type-B workers to retire early and some to retire late. We assume that type-A workers are more than willing to retire early and type-C workers are more than willing to retire late. These assumptions can be based on more primitive assumptions about differences in the additive disutility of labor. We do not spell these out exactly since precise limits depend on the structure of benefits—the division between lump sums and annuitized benefits.

We continue with the same four-period model with real social security benefits varying with retirement age but not age when receiving benefits. We continue to assume no savings before period 2, but now allow saving (but not borrowing) starting in period 2, with savings invested in perfect annuities. The model has full forward-looking behavior for all workers. This models the idea that some young people do not consider saving for retirement, but once retirement is available, they think rationally about saving. A more realistic structure would have saving start late in the career, but before eligibility for retirement. It would also recognize some failures of savings after reaching retirement age. But the assumed structure is a start on more complicated models. We continue to assume that both the interest rates and the utility discount rates are zero.

Everyone receives x_1 as net earnings in period 1. At the start of period 2, some people retire. They receive a lump sum, L_1, and an annuitized benefit, c_1. Those who work in period 2 receive a net wage, x_2, and an annuitized benefit,

c_2, starting in period 3. If we also allowed the government to give late retirees a lump sum at the end of period 2, such a lump sum would not be used. This follows from the fact that the net wage in period 2 is a (weakly) preferred payment. If all late retirees were saving out of their second-period wages, then the lump sum and the wage would be equivalent in their eyes and cost the government the same. If some of them are not saving, then, because of the liquidity constraint, they would gain from an increase in the wage, financed by an equal decrease in the lump sum. Since this would not decrease labor supply (and might increase it) the government cannot lose and may gain, given that the optimum has an implicit tax on work.

Utility if working is written as $u - a$, while utility if retired is written as v. We assume both functions are concave. As previously, p is the probability of worker p surviving to period 4; a, distributed as $F[a]$, is the additive disutility of labor in period 2 for type-B workers, and a_A and a_C are the additive disutilities of the other two types. With some abuse of notation, we use a_p to stand for the disutilities of all three types.

7.5   Individual Choice

With perfect annuities (no administrative costs and actuarially fair annuities at the individual level) everyone fully annuitizes, so there are no bequests. Moreover, with zero interest and discount rates, consumption levels will be the same in all periods covered by annuity purchase. If worker p spends A on annuities, this can purchase A in consumption in periods 2 or 3 or A/p in period 4. Since utility over the retirement periods is $v + v + pv$ for early retirees and $v + pv$ for late ones, the FOCs ensure equal

2048

consumption since there is not a binding liquidity constraint over retirement years.

A worker chooses between two plans. With no work in period 2, the lump sum at retirement and the annuitized benefit are combined to give equal consumption in the remaining periods of life. With a perfect annuity, the lump-sum L_1 can finance a per-period benefit for worker p of $L_1/(2+p)$. Thus, expected lifetime utility for worker p is[4]

$$V^1[c_1, L_1, p, a] = u[x]_1 - a + (2+p)v\left[c_1 + \frac{L_1}{2+p}\right]. \qquad (7.29)$$

Those who work in period 2 may find savings worthwhile in period 2. We denote optimal savings of worker p in period 2 by s_p^*. Note that savings depend on the survival probability but not the additive disutility of labor. Thus all type-B workers who retire at the same time save the same amount. For a worker choosing late retirement, we have[5]

---

4. Differentiating, we can examine how utility varies with survival probability.
$$\frac{\partial V^1[c_1, L_1, p]}{\partial p} = -\frac{\partial a_p}{\partial p} + v\left[c_1 + \frac{L_1}{2+p}\right] - \left(\frac{L_1}{2+p}\right)v'\left[c_1 + \frac{L_1}{2+p}\right].$$
Those with greater survivor probabilities have (weakly) lower disutility of work and a higher probability of enjoying the fourth period (which may or may not be positive) but face a higher price for consumption in period 4 if alive. Note that by concavity of v, we have
$$v\left[c_1 + \frac{L_1}{2+p}\right] - \left(\frac{L_1}{2+p}\right)v'\left[c_1 + \frac{L_1}{2+p}\right] \geq v[c_1].$$
5. Differentiating and using concavity, we can examine how utility varies with survival probability.
$$\frac{\partial V^2[x_2, c_2, p]}{\partial p} = -2\frac{\partial a_p}{\partial p} + v\left[c_2 + \frac{s_p^*}{1+p}\right] - \left(\frac{s_p^*}{1+p}\right)v\left[c_2 + \frac{s_p^*}{1+p}\right]$$
$$\geq -2\frac{\partial a_p}{\partial p} + v[c_2].$$

$$V^2[x_2, c_2, p, a] = u[x_1] - a$$

$$+ \text{Max}_s \, u[x_2 - s] - a + (1 + p)v\left[c_2 + \frac{s}{1 + p}\right].$$

$$(7.30)$$

Let us examine the pattern of savings. The first-order condition for the level of savings is

$$u'[x_2 - s_p^*] \geq v'\left[c_2 + \frac{s_p^*}{1 + p}\right], \qquad (7.31)$$

with equality if savings are positive. Note that either all late retirees save of none of them do, depending on the sign of $u'[x_2] - v'[c_2]$. Differentiating (7.31) when the FOC is satisfied as an equality, we have

$$\frac{\partial s_p^*}{\partial p} = \frac{-s_p^* v''\left[c_2 + \frac{s_p^*}{1 + p}\right] \Big/ (1 + p)^2}{-u''[x_2 - s_p^*] - v''\left[c_2 + \frac{s_p^*}{1 + p}\right]} > 0. \qquad (7.32)$$

That is, where savings are positive, savings are larger for the longer lived. This follows from their being "poorer" in the sense that they have to pay more for annuitized consumption in period 4.[6]

With a forward-looking retirement decision, the marginal second-period worker equates lifetime utility with the two plans. We assume that the marginal early retiree

---

6. If u and v differ only by a constant, when savings are positive, we have

$$x_2 - s_p^* = c_2 + \frac{s_p^*}{1 + p};$$

$$s_p^* = \frac{(x_2 - c_2)(1 + p)}{2 + p};$$

$$x_2 - s_p^* = \frac{x_2 + c_2(1 + p)}{2 + p}.$$

is a type-B worker with additive disutility denoted a^*.
Thus the marginal worker satisfies

$$V^1[c_1, L_1, p_B, a^*] = V^2[x_2, c_2, p_B, a^*]. \tag{7.33}$$

We assume that workers with shorter life expectancies
than type B retire early and those with longer life expectancies retire late. We do not analyze sufficient conditions
for this outcome, just assuming that the variation in the
disutility of labor is sufficient to give us the pattern of retirements assumed earlier. This is more complicated than
in the model without savings since the division of compensation between lump-sum and annuitized benefits im-
pacts workers with different life expectancies differently.

The implicit tax for worker p is

$$T[p] = n - x_2 - (1 + p)c_2 + L_1 + (2 + p)c_1. \tag{7.34}$$

To see how the implicit tax varies with life expectancy, we
differentiate T with respect to p:

$$\frac{dT[p]}{dp} = c_1 - c_2. \tag{7.35}$$

The implicit tax declines with life expectancy if the annuity is greater for late retirees than for early ones. I do not
know if this need be the case in an unconstrained optimum, but would be a plausible condition to add to the
problem.

7.6   Discrete-Types Model

As previously, we have three types with life expectancies
$p_A < p_B < p_C$. We denote the numbers of the types by f_A, 1,
and f_C. We examine optima for economies that have the

property that some type B's work in period 2 and some do not, with all A's early retirees and all C's late retirees. Depending on the relative magnitudes of these survival probabilities, we can get the different possibilities discussed earlier.

Consider the optimum with the constraint that benefits are fully annuitized. From this optimum, substituting some lump-sum benefit for some of the annuitized benefit, at a break-even rate for type-B workers raises the consumption of type-A workers since they face a more favorable annuity price. Since they have a social marginal utility of consumption that is larger than the Lagrange multiplier, this is a gain. Thus the optimum does not have all of benefits paid as annuities. Such a gain is available for further substitutions of a lump sum for annuitized benefits until type-A's marginal utility equals the Lagrange multiplier, or until the annuitized benefit is zero. That is, paying all of the benefit as a lump sum may be optimal.

For late retirees, we have the same possible outcomes. If all of the benefit is paid as an annuity (i.e., there is no savings), then the type-C workers have the same marginal utility of consumption as the late retirees among the type B's. By switching some resources from annuity to lump sum on a break-even basis for type-B workers, we lower the consumption of type-C workers and free up resources. Since the social marginal utility of consumption of these workers is less than the Lagrange multiplier, that is a gain. Thus we can conclude that the optimum does not have all of the benefit paid as an annuity. Whether all of the benefit should be paid as a lump sum depends on the marginal utility of consumption of the longer-lived at the consumption level they can finance in this way.

Thus, some use of lump sums is a way to lower the
consumption of the long-lived who are not marginal
workers and have low marginal utility of consumption
and a way to raise the consumption of the short-lived who
are not marginal workers and have high marginal utility
of consumption.[7]

To explore these results, we derive the conditions for
optimal benefits. First, we restate the optimization:

Maximize$_{x,c,L}$

$$f_A\left(u[x_1] - a_A + (2 + p_A)v\left[c_1 + \frac{L_1}{2 + p_A}\right]\right)$$

$$+ \beta\left(u[x_1] + (2 + p_B)v\left[c_1 + \frac{L_1}{2 + p_B}\right]\right) - \int_{a^*}^{\infty} adF[a]$$

$$+ (1 - \beta)\left(u[x_1] + u[x_2 - s_B^*] + (1 + p_B)v\left[c_2 + \frac{s_B^*}{1 + p_B}\right]\right)$$

$$- 2\int_0^{a^*} adF[a]$$

$$+ f_C\left(u[x_1] + u[x_2 - s_C^*] - 2a_C + (1 + p_C)v\left[c_2 + \frac{s_C^*}{1 + p_C}\right]\right)$$

7. We have assumed that the B workers are the marginal workers, with
A retiring early and C retiring late, without examining sufficient conditions on a_p. A complication is that retirement incentives may depend
on the mix between annuitized and lump-sum benefits and on how they
differ for early and late retirees. More use of lump sums for late retirees
makes late retirement more attractive for type-A workers and less attractive for type-C workers, and vice versa for early retirement benefits.
Whatever change in incentives occurs in this way can be overshadowed
by differences in the disutility of labor.

subject to $\quad E + x_1 - n + (f_A + \beta)L_1 + (f_A(2 + p_A)$

$\qquad + \beta(2 + p_B))c_1 + (1 - \beta + f_C)(x_2 - n)$

$\qquad + ((1 - \beta)(1 + p_B) + f_C(1 + p_C))c_2 \leq 0,$

$\qquad x_1 \geq 0; \ c_1 \geq 0; \ L_1 \geq 0; \ x_2 \geq 0; \ c_2 \geq 0,$

with a^* given by $(2 + p_B)v\left[c_1 + \dfrac{L_1}{2 + p_B}\right]$

$$= u[x_2 - s_B^*] - a^* + (1 + p_B)v\left[c_2 + \frac{s_B^*}{1 + p_B}\right]. \tag{7.36}$$

As above in (7.16), we define $\mu \equiv \lambda T[p_B]$ to simplify the expressions. Note that both x_1 and x_2 must be positive since otherwise some consumption is zero. But the other control variables may be zero. We have five FOCs for payment levels:

$$u'[x_1] - \lambda = 0 \tag{7.37}$$

$$f_A \frac{2 + p_A}{2 + p_B}\left(v'\left[c_1 + \frac{L_1}{2 + p_A}\right] - \lambda\right) + \beta\left(v'\left[c_1 + \frac{L_1}{2 + p_B}\right] - \lambda\right)$$

$$\leq \mu v'\left[c_1 + \frac{L_1}{2 + p_B}\right] \tag{7.38}$$

$$f_A\left(v'\left[c_1 + \frac{L_1}{2 + p_A}\right] - \lambda\right) + \beta\left(v'\left[c_1 + \frac{L_1}{2 + p_B}\right] - \lambda\right)$$

$$\leq \mu v'\left[c_1 + \frac{L_1}{2 + p_B}\right] \tag{7.39}$$

$$(1 - \beta)(u'[x_2 - s_B^*] - \lambda) + f_C(u'[x_2 - s_C^*] - \lambda) = -\mu u'[x_2 - s_B^*] \tag{7.40}$$

$$(1 - \beta)\left(v'\left[c_2 + \frac{s_B^*}{1 + p_B}\right] - \lambda\right)$$

$$+ f_C \frac{1 + p_C}{1 + p_B}\left(v'\left[c_2 + \frac{s_C^*}{1 + p_C}\right] - \lambda\right)$$

$$\leq - \mu v'\left[c_2 + \frac{s_B^*}{1 + p_B}\right] \qquad (7.41)$$

To analyze the division of benefits for early retirees, we consider the FOCs for their payments, (7.38) and (7.39). If there were no type A's, then lump-sum and annuitized early retirement benefits would be equivalent—equations (7.38) and (7.39) would be identical. This is not surprising since, with perfect annuity markets, a lump sum is fully equivalent to the annuitized benefit that can be bought by the lump sum. However, with the presence of some type-A workers, these two methods of payment are not equivalent since with worker B indifferent between payments, worker A prefers the lump sum. If both types of payments are used, (7.38) and (7.39) are both satisfied as equalities. This can happen if and only if at the optimum we have

$$v'\left[c_1 + \frac{L_1}{2 + p_A}\right] = \lambda = u'[x_1]. \qquad (7.42)$$

This would still give the pattern for type B of

$$v'\left[c_1 + \frac{L_1}{2 + p_B}\right] > \lambda = u'[x_1]. \qquad (7.43)$$

To consider possible corner conditions, note that with $c_1 > 0$ and $L_1 = 0$, we would have the result that $v'[c_1] > \lambda$. Thus, an equality in (7.38) would imply violating the inequality in (7.39). Thus the optimum has $L_1 > 0$. If the life expectancy of type-A workers is long enough (close to p_B), then we can have $c_1 = 0$. On the other hand, if their life expectancies are very short, so that with the benefit fully in a lump sum their consumption would be so high that it would be better to lower it, then this can be done by making some use of annuities for early retirees.

The presence of savings makes the other comparison a little more complicated. We turn to that now. For early retirees, the payment of a lump sum was separate from other variables. The equivalent action for late retirees is the payment of an amount in period 2 sufficient for positive savings to be carried over to later periods. As noted earlier, either both type-B and type-C workers save or both do not save. After showing similar results to those for early retirees assuming that savings are positive, we will show that assuming no savings leads to a contradiction.

Assume that both save in period 2. In this case, the workers have equated their marginal utilities in periods 2 and 3 and the two FOCs, (7.40) and (7.41), become

$$(1 - \beta)\left(v'\left[\frac{c_2 + s_B^*}{1 + p_B}\right] - \lambda\right) + f_C\left(v'\left[c_2 + \frac{s_C^*}{1 + p_C}\right] - \lambda\right)$$

$$= -\mu v'\left[c_2 + \frac{s_B^*}{1 + p_B}\right] \qquad (7.44)$$

$$(1 - \beta)\left(v'\left[c_2 + \frac{s_B^*}{1 + p_B}\right] - \lambda\right)$$

$$+ f_C \frac{1 + p_C}{1 + p_B}\left(v'\left[c_2 + \frac{s_C^*}{1 + p_C}\right] - \lambda\right)$$

$$\leq -\mu v'\left[c_2 + \frac{s_B^*}{1 + p_B}\right]. \qquad (7.45)$$

Since $x_2 > 0$, (7.44) is an equality. The analysis is similar to that of the early retirees above. Thus we have a positive annuity when both are saving if and only if (7.44) and (7.45) are both satisfied with equalities. This implies

$$v'\left[c_2 + \frac{s_C^*}{1+p_C}\right] = \lambda = u'[x_1]. \tag{7.46}$$

This would still give the pattern for type B that

$$v'\left[c_2 + \frac{s_B^*}{1+p_B}\right] < \lambda = u'[x_1]. \tag{7.47}$$

Otherwise, with $v'[c_2 + (s_C^*/(1+p_C))] < \lambda$, we can have $c_2 = 0$, with (7.40) rewritten as

$$(1-\beta)\left(v'\left[\frac{s_B^*}{1+p_B}\right] - \lambda\right) + f_C\left(v'\left[\frac{s_C^*}{1+p_C}\right] - \lambda\right)$$
$$= -\mu v'\left[\frac{s_B^*}{1+p_B}\right], \tag{7.48}$$

and (7.41) becoming

$$(1-\beta)\left(v'\left[\frac{s_B^*}{1+p_B}\right] - \lambda\right) + f_C\frac{1+p_C}{1+p_B}\left(v'\left[\frac{s_C^*}{1+p_C}\right] - \lambda\right)$$
$$< -\mu v'\left[\frac{s_B^*}{1+p_B}\right]. \tag{7.49}$$

The remaining case is that neither save. In this case, the FOCs (7.40) and (7.41) are

$$(1-\beta+f_C)(u'[x_2] - \lambda) = -\mu u'[x_2] \tag{7.50}$$

$$\left(1-\beta+f_C\frac{(1+p_C)}{(1+p_B)}\right)(v'[c_2] - \lambda) = -\mu v'[c_2]. \tag{7.51}$$

Solving for the marginal utilities, we have

$$(1 - \beta + f_C + \mu)u'[x_2] = (1 - \beta + f_C)\lambda \qquad (7.52)$$

$$\left(1 - \beta + f_C \frac{1 + p_C}{1 + p_B} + \mu\right)v'[c_2] = \left(1 - \beta + f_C \frac{1 + p_C}{1 + p_B}\right)\lambda. \quad (7.53)$$

This would imply

$$\frac{u'[x_2]}{v'[c_2]} = \frac{(1 - \beta + f_C)\left(1 - \beta + f_C + \mu + f_C \dfrac{p_C - p_B}{1 + p_B}\right)}{\left(1 - \beta + f_C + f_C \dfrac{p_C - p_B}{1 + p_B}\right)(1 - \beta + f_C + \mu)} < 1,$$

$$(7.54)$$

which is a contradiction to the absence of savings. We conclude that some lump sum is always used in the sense that there is positive savings.

7.7   Conclusion

I have not considered what would happen with savings in private group annuities or in bonds instead of annuities. In the former case, there would be an endogenous price of annuities that would vary with the set of workers who choose late retirement and with the levels of savings. In the latter case, we need to monitor bequests. There are interesting alternative models of the allocation of estates, the simplest of which would have 100 percent taxation of estates. Without an overlapping-generations (OLG) model, we could also consider the allocation to surviving members of this cohort. Then we would want to reflect the issues of how the allocation differs across life expectancies from an equal allocation. And we would want to consider the lumpiness in allocation, as opposed to a smooth allocation to everyone. These alternative patterns would affect the marginal social value of induced change in period 3 savings, which determine estates. As I have said repeatedly, analysis with just one type of worker illustrates some of the economic forces at work. But models with several kinds of worker behavior are important for testing the results in simpler models and getting closer to reality. It is also relevant that there are no wealth differences and so no early retirees with large wealth, high consumption, and low social marginal utility of consumption.

8   Pension Insurance Reform with a Focus on Germany

Systems to provide pensions need to be adjusted from time to time. This is true of public systems and is also true of private systems. Sometimes the need arises from a mismatch between finances and benefits under existing rules. Sometimes the need arises from a mismatch between system design and the social needs that pensions are trying to meet. This chapter begins by discussing pension insurance reform in general terms. Then I turn to some specific issues here in Germany, including the adjustment of benefits for the age of retirement and the determination of survivor benefits for the elderly.[1]

Given the need for periodic reform, there are two basic questions. How frequently is changing the system likely to be seriously considered? And what circumstances are likely to shape the actions or inactions at such times? For a public system, these are questions of political economy,

---

1. There is a literature on reform issues in Germany. For some examples of this literature, see the Symposium on the Reform of the Retirement Provision System: Homburg (2000), Breyer (2000), Schmähl (2000), Börsch-Supan (2000b), Thum and von Weizsäcker (2000). Other references include Börsch-Supan and Schnabel (1999), Börsch-Supan (2000a), Schnabel (1998, 1999), and Wissenschaftlicher Beirat beim Bundesministerium für Wirtschaft (1998).

of the interaction between the workings of the pension system and the political process.[2] I start with two presumptions. First, a system to provide retirement income should not be changed very often. And second, when it is changed, it is best to have significant lead time before substantial changes take effect. These presumptions come from the need of both retirees and older workers to rely on the system at a time in life when it is more difficult to adapt to changed circumstances.[3] So, this conclusion is especially true for decreases in benefits relative to what was in previous legislation. However, the ability to delay implementation while preserving fairness is dependent upon passing legislation well in advance of short-run fiscal needs. Thus, a key issue is how to get government to address future fiscal problems that are not imminent crises. On the other hand, it is good to have pressure to review how the system is working from time to time— every decade or so. Changing circumstances will alter the desirability of particular rules. In addition, a time of revisiting the system is a time when reformers can try to change elements that were poor designs previously.

From this perspective, it is important that the political process not find it easy to change the pension rules for reasons that do not relate to retirement issues. And it is helpful if there is pressure on the political process to react to future needs well before there is extreme financial pressure. A country that is changing pension rules annually is not doing a good job.

---

2. For a discussion of the political economy of social security reform in the United States, see Diamond (1999a).

3. In addition, greater confidence in future benefits generated by early responses to future problems increases the willingness of workers to pay "contributions" and decreases the distortionary effects of such taxes.

8.1   Insulation from Too-Frequent Changes

The pension system should be insulated from the year-to-year state of the government budget, although it needs to be responsive to the overall (long-run) state of fiscal capacity. To contribute to political insulation, it is common to earmark particular revenues for financing pensions.[4] And it is usually a payroll tax that is so earmarked as here in Germany—with an earmarked payroll tax of 19.3 percent (half on employees and half on employers) up to a maximum earnings level of 103,200 DM per year (as of 2000). But the payroll tax revenue here is not sufficient to cover current benefit payments. Nearly 30 percent of the current benefit flow is financed from general revenues, with several tax increases having been legislated to help cover this expense. And, under current legislation, the need for general revenues will grow substantially as the baby boom generation retires. That is, currently legislated benefits can not be financed by the resources

---

4. It is common to have part of payroll taxes earmarked for financing retirement benefits. This link between taxes and benefits serves two purposes. One is the incidence of taxes to pay for benefits. Assuming there is not a full adjustment in other sources of tax revenue, the use of a payroll tax, typically proportional up to a ceiling, places the tax burden on the labor market and determines the degree of progressivity with earned income. The second purpose is to affect the political process. This has two parts. On one hand, it makes it more difficult to cut benefits below what can be financed from current and past payroll taxes because of the sense of political entitlement that comes from paying. On the other hand, the link limits the success of demands for larger benefits because of the need to finance them in a visible way. When a less-than-fully-funded system is immature this latter effect is not present, while once a system is mature the former effect is unlikely to matter. This connection is particularly important when there is a successful mechanism to make the public, and the political process, aware of future costs. Actuarial projections attempt to play that role.

earmarked for social security (from the payroll tax[5]) plus a continuation of roughly the same level of general revenues now being transferred. Moreover, the fiscal needs are pressing since the rise in costs is not too distant by the standards of how retirement income systems should be changed.

With so much reliance on general revenues, there is a strong temptation at times of budgetary stringency to make repeated small cuts in benefits in ways that are not very visible. Succumbing to such temptation results in a system that works less well.

One approach to adding insulation is to expand earmarked taxation (not necessarily the payroll tax) in order to build the tradition of separation of the two budgets (both ways). Budget separation needs to be ingrained in the political process; it is not sufficient merely to have legally separate accounting. Separation has two effects—it keeps up pressure to balance revenues and benefits in pensions, and it keeps down pressure to adjust benefits because of fiscal needs elsewhere. Another source of insulation used by some countries is to have reserve funds to protect benefits. For example, before it embarked on its current pattern of partial (and probably transitory) advance funding, the U.S. Social Security system had a goal of a reserve fund equal to one year's expenditures. A reserve fund of approximately one month's expenditures is needed just to have a smooth cash flow and is the practice here in Germany. A year's fund, in addition to being a round number, represents enough financing to get through an extended recession, although not a large depression.

---

5. One percent of the VAT and part of the gasoline tax are earmarked as well.

In an advanced economy with easy government access to the capital market, an earmarked reserve fund (beyond the needs purely for cash flow purposes) is not necessary for the government to be able to pay benefits. Rather, the purpose is political—to help the political process to adhere to good long-run strategy, to make it harder to follow short-run temptations to make changes in the cash flow that do not conform to long-run planning. Governments need accounting rules to have visibility in their actions. Separating pension financing from the rest of the budget is a good example of such a rule.

While such accounting rules can help in general, any specific accounting rule may tend to hinder some good policies or encourage some poor ones. As an example, let us consider the Maastricht restrictions on debt relative to GDP. The restriction is in terms of explicit debt, ignoring the implicit debt inherent in currently legislated retirement systems.[6] This is a striking omission because of the

---

6. One should not simply view implicit social security debt as the same as explicit contractual debt. The ability of government to adjust the debts without overwhelming cost is very different in the two cases. In either case, a government can cut other expenditures or raise taxes, both of which are politically difficult. Beyond that lies the differences. Repudiating debt has serious consequences. But social security systems can sometimes be adjusted without disruptive consequences. In particular, we have the possibility of current legislation of changes that start having effects well into the future as a way to reduce an implicit debt obligation that is viewed as too large. Moreover, the social understanding about these two forms of debt are different.

Explicit debt is meant to be paid, although inflation is a way of modifying the real value of nominal debt in ways that may not have been contemplated by the lenders. In contrast, defined benefit social security systems are set up in ways that will almost surely require some adaptation over time. To the extent that the public understands that periodic adjustments are part of the inherent design, and to the extent that the public is made genuinely aware of the real needs of the system, then

general pattern in Europe, indeed more generally, to have implicit pension debt that is larger than the explicit debt. Thus, by itself, separated accounting serves as a disincentive to accumulate earmarked reserves, whether in government debt or other assets, since reducing the implicit debt does not affect the Maastricht conditions. Yet, when the Netherlands decided to start a separate fund to help finance retirement benefits for the baby boom generation, the Maastricht rules were modified to count such reserves as a decrease in debt outstanding. So rules have their role but are not ironclad constraints.

8.2 Stimulus for Legislating Change before a Crisis

If there is a great likelihood that future revenues will not be adequate for future benefits, it is clearly advantageous to make changes well in advance. There are three reasons for taking actions well in advance. One is that the sooner the action is taken, the greater the flow of benefits and revenues that can be adjusted. As time goes by, one cannot go back in order to have had lower benefits or higher revenues. More scope for action can make the out-

---

suitably designed and executed adjustments are part of the implicit social contract, not a breach of that contract. What is a breach is a badly designed change, given the expectations built into the system. Indeed, even defined contributions systems should be altered from time to time. So these two types of debt are quite distinct because of the different abilities to change the quantities outstanding.

But that does not have the reverse implication that the implicit debt is irrelevant for the future economic health of a country. Indeed that debt is important for two reasons. It is a sign of some of the financial difficulties the political process will have to face in some form. And, when the projections are believable, they are a sign to the public of the need for government response, a recognition that is essential if government is to move toward balance in such a large and sensitive program.

come better, in terms of efficiency or fairness or both. By having a larger base of taxes and benefits to change, the changes can be smaller in percentage terms.

A second reason for early change is the enhanced ability of some people to react to change. It is better to tell a 54-year-old that benefits need to be cut starting in eleven years than to wait ten years and then tell a 64-year-old that benefits need to be cut starting the following year. Advance warning of changes will help some people make better adaptations. To help adaptation, a move to lower benefits in the future should be accompanied by enhanced opportunities for individuals to save on their own for their own retirements.

A third advantage of early action is that it is politically easier the earlier it is (at least until a crisis requires change and so alters the political discussion). No one likes to deliver bad news, particularly not officials hoping to be reelected. If the bad news is in the form of a projection, then there is the risk that the political competition will deny the bad news and the need to do something about it. Thus, there is a tendency for pensions to be adjusted only when a crisis is imminent. So there is a need to find ways to encourage early legislated responses. After all, cutting benefits starting in twenty years should not risk as much politically as cutting them starting in ten years.

The same goes for legislating future tax increases. Indeed, until 1990 it was a hallmark of U.S. Social Security to have future tax increases always on the books. When the date of a tax increase came along, the increase was sometimes delayed if revenue needs turned out less than had been anticipated. And politicians got to posture that the tax increase would be repealed, but it never was—delayed sometimes but not repealed. This asymmetry in the political process—that it is politically easy to cut taxes or raise benefits, while the reverse is difficult—is why it is important to legislate financial cushions well in advance. The further in the future is the impact of the legislation, the less the asymmetry in the process. There is less at stake in both directions when the effects do not happen for a long time.

If early legislation is to stand a chance, the public needs to go along with the view that some advance action is desirable. So a central question is how to have an institution that can influence the public in this direction. In the United States, even though there is some debate about the severity of the long-run fiscal problem, that debate is in a setting where the public recognizes the importance of the issue and the value of projections of costs and benefits, even though the future is uncertain. The history that has made this work is the presence of a highly respected Office of the Actuary in Social Security. This government agency is staffed by professionals and regularly reviewed by panels of outside experts—both economists and actuaries. This review process helps the professional staff resist political pressures and helps convince the rest of the government and the public of the high quality of the annual reports.

How can widely accepted projections be generated? Wide acceptance can happen in a country that has its own independent office making projections, provided that they have sufficient independence and enough history to have earned credibility. If not already present, then wide acceptance probably cannot be built up quickly. With social security reform so pressing in so many European countries, this suggests the creation of an international institution to provide projections. An international organization, such as the IMF or the World Bank, could provide estimates or, even better, fund the provision of estimates by independent bodies. The European Community should take on such a role. Indeed, the World Bank should do this more widely. The politics can be kept more limited by oversight of such an independent agency by professional associations of actuaries in different countries. While these projections are called "actuarial," they contain a good deal of economics as well, and require economic inputs as well as demographic ones.

8.3   Balancing Benefits and Revenues

The retirement of the baby boomers will stress the retirement income system here in Germany. Even after the boomers have retired, we expect to have improving mortality among the elderly. Therefore, costs for retirement income would continue to rise even if the population stabilized. Germany might be able to choose to simply live with this pattern, having steadily rising taxes to finance retirement benefits. However, the prospect of a continuing trend to steadily higher taxes, which are already high, casts doubt on the sense of such an approach. Without choosing among them, I want to lay out some aspects of the alternatives, assuming that some of the response will happen with both revenues and benefits.

A government with outstanding debt and the ability to borrow more has a wide choice of when to collect extra revenues. That is, a given present discounted value of the excess of future benefit payments over future revenues can be covered with higher revenues spread in different patterns over the different years. The obvious fact is that for permanent tax increases, the sooner the tax rate increase the smaller it has to be to raise the same aggregate revenue. This observation is not restricted to merely covering the payment flows in the early years. Beyond that, earmarked revenue increases can be used to cover later benefit payments. This is most readily done by having an earmarked fund, meant to be used solely for the retirement income program. Such an earmarked fund might hold government debt, reducing the extent of government borrowing from the public. Or the fund might be invested in other assets to some degree, with less reduction in the government's borrowing.[7] For example, the Netherlands is putting some general revenues into a fund holding government debt, a fund that is not to be used before 2020, and then used for retirement benefits. The U.S. Social Security system has been running annual cash surpluses from the portion of the payroll tax earmarked for retirement income. This has built up a fund, which earns interest. In the future, ongoing interest earnings and the stock of assets itself can be used to pay benefits. The Clinton administration proposed that part of this fund be invested in private assets although there has been no action.

So, one issue for Germany is to select the time shape of whatever total revenue increase is chosen for financing future retirement benefits. In addition, if the revenue increases are specifically earmarked, then there is a portfolio choice to be made. The connection between building a fund and increasing national savings is also important. That link depends primarily on the choice of other fiscal actions that are changed as a consequence of legislating a

---

7. If it were to come to pass that there was no government debt outstanding, an extraordinarily unlikely event, then such a fund would necessarily have to find other assets.

fund buildup. It also depends on how private savers respond. Improved pension financing will add to national savings to the extent that an improved fiscal position for pensions is not offset by a worsening fiscal position on the rest of the government budget. Higher national savings will increase future income available for both workers and pensioners.

While one could have payroll tax rates that vary with age (and Switzerland does), there are clear administrative advantages in having a uniform payroll tax. Thus tax rates are plausibly changed by date, not by cohort or date of birth. On the benefit side, the choice of base is more salient. Put simply, should benefit cuts be date-specific or cohort-specific? Several countries have gone the route of using cohort-specific benefit determination by relating benefits to the life expectancy of a cohort once it reaches eligibility for retirement benefits. Sweden has gone this route in what is called a Notional Defined Contribution system. A cohort in Sweden with longer life expectancy would receive lower monthly benefits, similar to how an insurance company would price an annuity (based on interest rates and life expectancy). There are two sides to such an approach as opposed to simply reducing the benefit formula over time (preferably straightforwardly, but possibly by fiddling with the indexing rules in ways that are hard for the public to understand). On the one hand, it can be argued that retirees of different ages who had the same earnings relative to average earnings when they worked should receive the same benefits. On the other hand, it can be argued that retirees who are in a cohort with longer life expectancy should have lower benefits so that there is not so much transfer from shorter-lived, earlier cohorts to longer-lived, later ones. One advantage

of cohort-specific rules is that once a cohort's initial benefits are set, then the indexing will keep net benefits up
with net earnings (the basis for indexing benefits in force
here in Germany). Otherwise, phasing in benefit cuts by
date reduces benefits for the already retired (relative to
net earnings) at the same time that it reduces initial benefits for newly retiring cohorts. That is, retirees might prefer a lower initial benefit that is then stable relative to the
net-wage index rather than a greater initial benefit that
then declines relative to the index. There is power in the
arguments on both sides, and what needs to be recognized is that this is a choice that needs to be made.

8.4 Retirement Age

It is common to refer to three options for dealing with
pension system fiscal imbalance—more revenues, lower
benefits, and a higher retirement age. I want to explain
why I focus on just the first two options, not all three.
Two different roles exist for retirement ages in pension
benefit rules, quite separate from whatever mandatory
retirement rules are adopted by employers. Whatever is
done with benefit rules, it would be good to revisit the
issue of mandatory retirement ages. One role for a retirement age in benefit rules is the age associated with what
are called "full benefits"—the age for which the benefit
factor is one, with entry adjustment reductions for earlier
retirement and entry adjustment increases for later ones.
Under current law, this age will be 65 for sufficiently later
cohorts (the lower age for women is being slowly increased to 65). If this age is increased, then this is fully
equivalent to a particular benefit cut—there is no difference. To see this, let us consider the effect of a two-year

increase in this age from 65 to 67.[8] For someone who retires at 65, benefits are reduced by 7.2 percent because of retiring two years before the age for full benefits. Without the change in the age for full benefits, there was not this benefit cut. Someone might say that this person could work longer and restore the benefit cut. Working until age 67 would both increase the number of earnings points for benefit determination and remove the 7.2 percent reduction for early retirement.[9] (Delaying the start of benefits until age 67 would have the latter effect, without continuing to work.) But this option would be there even if the age for full benefits did not change. By working until age 67 when the age for full benefits is 65, a worker receives a 7.2 percent larger benefit. So changing the age for full benefits is a benefit cut, plain and simple, and should be evaluated in those terms—it does not represent a third option.[10]

The story is very different when we consider changing the age at which retirement benefits can *first* be claimed.

---

8. In the United States, 1983 legislation slowly phased in an increase in the age for full benefits, called the Normal Retirement Age, from 65 to 67.

9. Earnings points are defined as the ratio of earnings subject to tax to the average earnings in that year. Earnings points are also given for nonearning time including, for example, child care, home nursing, unemployment, education. Some low earnings points have been increased. Earnings points are then summed over an entire career. Benefits for a retired worker equal the product of earnings points, a factor for type of pension and age of claiming, and an aggregate factor that indexes net of tax benefits to net of tax wages.

10. Note that this method of reducing benefits results in larger percentage cuts for workers retiring earlier. An individual's benefits are proportional to the factor $(1 + .036(Age - N))$, where Age is the age at which benefits start and N is the age for full benefits. Thus the percentage change in benefits from an increase in N is $-.036/(1 + .036(Age - N))$. This percentage change is smaller in absolute value for larger values of Age.

For workers who do not get disability or unemployment benefits as a substitute, ineligibility for retirement benefits does reduce the cost of benefits in that year. However, if benefits start one year later because the eligibility age is one year later, then benefits are larger when they do start, because the entry adjustment reduction is smaller. If the entry adjustment factor were actuarially fair, then there would be no saving to the expected present discounted value budget constraint of the government. The adjustment, however, is smaller than would be actuarially fair. So forcing a worker to wait a year does save the government some money, but only to the extent that a 3.6 percent change in benefits is too small a change for delayed retirement. Choice of the age at which benefits can first be claimed should be based primarily on consideration of the needs and proclivities of retirees, not overall financial needs. The closer the benefit adjustment to actuarially fair, the less the relevance for the overall budget, and good incentives should not be too far from actuarially fair.

8.5 Adjustment of Pensions for Early and Late Retirement

In order to have reasonable incentives to continue work past the age of first eligibility for benefits, it is common for retirement income systems to increase benefits for a delayed start.[11] It is also common for governments to legislate a simple linear formula for doing this, although sometimes the formulae are different before and after the age for full benefits. A linear formula is not a good one.

---

11. It is also important to have sufficient stringency in the standards for eligibility for disability and unemployment benefits.

As workers age, mortality probabilities rise. Therefore, to offset a delay of benefits, it is necessary to give larger increases in benefits the older the worker who is delaying the start of benefits. In contrast, a linear formula gives a decreasing percentage increase in benefits as a worker ages.[12] It would be good to move away from this linear formula since it does not make sense to reduce the incentive to work as workers age. Indeed, to the extent that workers are forward looking, there is a case for increasing the adjustment as they age, above and beyond the need to adjust for increased mortality.

8.6   Benefit Formula

Retirement benefits here are primarily related proportionally to the earnings subject to tax, and so to earnings up to the earnings limit. That is, generally, someone with a history of earnings twice as high (but still below the limit) pays twice as much tax and gets twice as large a benefit. This is not completely accurate since in the past some low earnings years have had their points increased as part of fighting poverty. In addition, there are credits given for some nonearning times, including child care and home nursing care, unemployment, and education. So, the system is not fully proportional. Nevertheless, it is in stark contrast with some other systems. The United States uses a highly progressive benefit formula—benefits are a higher fraction of earnings for low earners than for high earners. The higher life expectancy of male higher earners

---

12. An individual's benefits are proportional to the factor $(1 + .036(Age - 65))$, where Age is the age at which benefits start. Thus the percentage change in benefits for a delayed start is $.036(1 + .036(Age - 65))$. This percentage change declines with Age.

compared to male lower earners in the United States off-sets approximately half of the progressivity in the benefit formula when considered on a lifetime basis. The Nether-lands gives a flat benefit to all, workers or not, varying only by household status—single or married.[13] While the presence of an income tax introduces some progressivity for those whose benefits end up taxed, this approach does not seem to do enough about income distribution among the elderly generally. Without knowing any of the history that led to the result, it strikes me that the taxation of benefits here is very low relative to the usual public finance considerations.

In contrast, poverty is well addressed by pensions to-gether with separate programs. The combination of pro-grams has left very little poverty among the elderly in Germany. I wish the same were true in the United States. Preservation of this successful outcome should remain an integral part of the coming reforms.

8.7 Survivor Benefits

Pension systems (along with direct antipoverty programs) are concerned with helping to keep the elderly out of poverty. But there is a widely recognized second concern —to smooth or avoid drops in living standards when a worker retires or, later on, dies. This is a concern over a wide range of the income distribution and is not just a poverty issue. In considering survivor benefits, I focus now on replacement rates rather than poverty.

Consider an older couple, both retired (whether both of them worked previously or just one). Many older couples

---

13. Both countries also rely on substantial private provision of pensions by employers.

above the poverty line are living primarily on pension benefits (along with whatever housing they may own). A key question is how large a benefit either of them would need as a survivor in order to preserve the same economic standard of living that they previously enjoyed as a couple. Worldwide, there is recognition that there are economies of scale in living as a couple, and the survivor would need more than half of what the couple had. Perhaps 60 percent would be adequate, although many analysts and governments seem to think that 70 percent would be better. For example, the publicly provided benefit for a single person in the Netherlands over age 65 is 70 percent of the benefits for a couple.[14] I have not seen anyone gather arguments as to whether a surviving husband or a surviving wife would need a larger fraction in order to preserve the standard of living. So, I will stay with the natural presumption that there is symmetry in needs.[15]

From this perspective, the current German survivor benefit is not terrible, but not as well designed as it could be. The benefit rule is not symmetric within a couple and the survivor's benefit varies with the past relative earnings of husband and wife across couples with the same total earnings. These criticisms have also been leveled at social security in the United States, where academic commentators are pressing for changes in the design of survivor benefits to relate survivor benefits to the benefits that had been received by the couple. In both the United States and Germany, the design of survivor benefits is a legacy

---

14. This is the Algemene Ouderdomswet (AOW).

15. On the one hand, on average women have more experience in household tasks, while, on the other hand, men have greater remarriage prospects. There is also no apparent case for arguing that the survivor fraction needed would be different if before retirement both rather than just one of them had worked.

of a time when one-earner couples were dominant. As female labor force attachment has risen, it is time to reconsider this structure, paying more attention to the labor market incentives for women.

Before turning to this issue in detail, let me clear up another. Some people never marry. Others are divorced or widowed well before retirement age. Thus, any pension system needs rules distinguishing how it treats retired couples from how it treats individuals who are one-person households. This suggests that survivor benefits can be financed, in part, out of lower benefits for a couple than would be the case if no survivor benefits were to be paid. And they can be financed in part out of lower benefits for an earner who survives a lower-earning spouse. Since the system ignores differences in life expectancy among individuals (women living longer than men on average and higher-earning men living longer than lower-earning men, on average), full financing of survivor benefits out of lower worker benefits might be excessive. Conceptually an issue is how much to think of the system in terms of workers or in terms of workers and their families as a single unit. The central point is that there is no necessary link between the structure of survivor benefits and the relative treatment of couples and never-married individuals.

Let us consider how the survivor benefit is determined here, assuming both husband and wife are fully retired. It is easy to describe the situation for a one-earner couple. If the earner dies, the survivor gets 60 percent of what the couple had. If the nonearner dies, the survivor gets 100 percent of what the couple had. A couple could offset this asymmetry by using part of the benefit while both are alive to purchase life insurance on the now-retired earner.

Should the earner die first, the life insurance benefit could then be used to purchase an annuity for the survivor. By choosing the right level of life insurance, the couple can arrange the same income for either survivor. But the whole point of government-provided pension insurance is not to rely on individuals and the private market to make such arrangements. Many couples never would, and the market is inherently more expensive than building the right pattern into the structure of pension and survivor benefits.[16]

The government proposal to allow earnings points to be split 50-50 between husband and wife is a move in the direction of enhanced opportunity for symmetry.[17] Choices made by couples are very sensitive to both the selection of a default and the procedure for change. Allowing a couple to request a 50-50 split will generate different outcomes for many couples than will having a 50-50 split unless they apply to revert to the allocation of points individually earned. That is, opt-in systems and opt-out systems give different aggregate outcomes, even when the set of choices is the same in the two cases. Moreover, in the United States, a rule requiring a notarized signature by a spouse if there is no survivor benefit in private defined benefit (or annuitized defined contribution) pensions had an effect on the extent of survivor benefits chosen.

---

16. Of course, government programs require considerable uniformity, retaining value for the ability to change the pattern through market transactions.

17. The change in the total expected benefits as a consequence of 50-50 splitting depends on the life expectancy of husband and wife and on the relative size of the exempt amount before survivor pensions are reduced for the presence of own pensions.

There can be reduction of the survivor benefit because of the own-pension benefit of the survivor. This implies that the replacement rates among couples with the same total earnings are different for different divisions of the earnings history between husband and wife. The rule is that there is an exempt amount, DM 1282.51 per month (in 2000) in the West and DM 1115.66 in the East. If the benefit of the survivor is below the exempt amount, there is no offset. For survivors with positive pension benefits but below the exempt amount, the replacement rate is more than 60 percent because they get 60 percent of the deceased spouse's benefit along with 100 percent of their own pension. However, if the survivor has a pension above the exempt amount, then the survivor benefit is reduced by 40 percent of the excess of the own-pension over the exempt amount. This can reduce the survivor fraction to as low as 50 percent.[18] For example, if husband and wife have the same number of earnings points and that is at least twice as large as the exempt amount, then there is no survivor benefit and the survivor receives 50 percent of what the couple had.

Given changing labor force patterns, this is likely to be more of an issue in the future. In the United States, where social security gives the survivor between one-half and two-thirds of what the couple had (apart from actuarial adjustments), longitudinal data reveals that on average

---

18. Expressed as an equation, in terms of the earning points of husband, H, and wife, W, and the exempt amount expressed in earnings points, E, a surviving wife would get a total benefit, BW, which satisfies

$$BW = W + \text{Max}\{0, 0.6H - 0.4\text{Max}\{0, W - E\}\}$$

$$= W - 0.4\text{Max}\{0, W - E\} + \text{Max}\{0.4(W - E), 0.6H\}.$$

The law is symmetric by gender.

widows have a drop in income relative to needs of roughly 30 percent (Holden and Zick 1998). I do not know of any similar German study. Thus I think that the structure of survivor benefits for the elderly needs to be changed—with the benefits for a survivor related consistently to the benefits that had been received by the couple. To the extent that couples would choose to split their earnings points 50-50 if they had the opportunity, these differences could be less important. But not all couples will make such a choice.

Considering the replacement ratio for a survivor and recognizing that many couples would not split their earnings points even if they could, the government proposal to reduce the survivor benefit from 60 percent to 55 percent of the worker benefit seems to me to be going in the wrong direction. In the long run, benefits do need to be cut. Any cut in workers' benefits automatically is a cut in survivor benefits as well. Thus to also cut the survivor fraction is to cut survivor benefits by a larger percentage than worker benefits are cut. For example, to reduce the replacement rate for a worker from 70 percent to 64 percent is an 8.6 percent decrease in benefits. For a widow with no earnings points, a survivor benefit of 55 percent of a 64 percent replacement rate is a 16.2 percent cut in the survivor benefit (compared with 60 percent of 70 percent). I do not see how a proposal to cut survivor benefits by 16.2 percent while cutting worker benefits by only 8.6 percent can be justified. A similar argument would apply to making the income testing of survivor benefits more stringent. It is important to consider survivor benefits in terms of suitable replacement rates generally, and not narrowly as part of antipoverty efforts.

8.8 Concluding Remarks

In this chapter, I have argued for the need to build an institution to help the public obtain a realistic view of the set of alternatives. This might make it easier to take action sooner in order to put costs and benefits on a comfortable track. I have also argued for more incentives to continue working past age 65 by increasing the entry adjustment factor. And I have argued for a rethinking of survivor benefits to relate them to the benefits that had been received by the couple.

9   Theory and Policy

This chapter provides a perspective on the link between chapter 8 and the earlier chapters. Chapter 8 was a discussion of issues directly relevant for policy, while the earlier chapters discussed basic theory. In this chapter, I briefly consider the back-and-forth between theory and policy. It is indeed a back-and-forth. Some applied theoretical analyses are meant to illuminate issues in policy choices. In turn, public policy institutions motivate the selection of issues for theoretical analysis. Moreover, discussions of policy highlight the issues that are critical in policy design and so focus the choice of models for theoretical analysis.

I begin with some observations on the approach of economists generally. Economists differ from other social scientists, and non–social scientists, in a number of important ways. One is our attention to incentives and their effects. The second is our awareness of general equilibrium. Theory in these two areas is important for informing the design of both social insurance and social assistance programs. I also want to touch on political economy, a subject in its infancy as measured by its state of development, but very important, nevertheless.

9.1 Incentives

If one didn't believe that incentives had effects, one could evaluate the consequences of (implicitly or explicitly) taking money away from some people and giving it to others by simply looking at the transfers and the consumption changes from payments and receipts. However, economists believe that there are significant behavioral responses, in both consumption patterns and in labor supply. We think that work varies with the level of other income and with the return to working. So the first step after describing transfers is to think about how people will change their behavior when government programs change their range of opportunities.

The relationship between government programs and behavior is complicated. Any single program will affect many types of behavior, not just hours worked, but also intensity, risk taking, career choice, human capital accumulation, migration, and so on. Conversely, any behavioral decision will be affected by many programs; each choice, such as labor supply, depends on all the programs that affect how much work increases incomes at that time and later. For example, when thinking about the incentive effects of multipillar social insurance systems (and all systems are multipillar), one can not ignore the interactions among systems. Indeed the correct way to analyze the incentive effects of a multipillar system is by integrating the pillars and examining the implied incentives of the equivalent single pillar system. The purpose of multipillar systems is to help the thinking and talking and politics of the design of incentives; the purpose is not to have some pillar have good effects when considered in isolation.

But evaluating incentives is just the first step in the design of social systems. Knowing, estimating, or guessing how people will respond to incentives is just an input in the design of incentives, which is a difficult and unavoidable design problem. The problem is unavoidable since every program affects incentives. The major source of the difficulty of design has been referred to in several vocabularies. I will use an optimization vocabulary, although the same considerations occur when choosing between two alternatives, neither of which is necessarily a formal optimum. The problem has been referred to as a double maximization problem in that the maximization of the analyst's evaluation of outcomes is done subject to the constraint that individuals will be maximizing against the constraints that are put before them. Put differently, the set of individual behavioral responses gives a set of constraints on the design of social systems that is complicated and difficult to use.

This difficulty is present when we consider simple linear incentive systems but becomes even harder to think about when we recognize nonlinearities. Like multipillar approaches, nonlinearities are pervasive in actual government choices. In thinking about linear systems, such as a value-added tax (VAT) or a cigarette tax or a flat pension, one averages the gains and losses across people, with these gains and losses having the same structure of revenue, income distribution, and efficiency effects for everyone. A nonlinear system is harder to think about because of the trade-off between higher disincentives for some people and the revenue effects coming from people higher up the income or wealth scale. In other words, one can no longer think in terms of an average of simple representative taxpayers or benefit recipients. And that is more difficult.

Any realistic policy has disincentive effects. Pointing this out does not end the discussion, as some opponents of programs would have us think. Even pointing out the presence of very high disincentive effects on some of the population does not end the discussion. For example, very high implicit marginal tax rates typically separate people on welfare from the rest of the population. The alternatives to such high rates are some combination of lower benefits for those with the lowest incomes and higher tax rates on people with much higher incomes. Optimal tax considerations show that the optimal pattern of disincentives may include high disincentives for some. There is a trade-off between discouraging work among the moderately poor and having more revenue for the very poor. This is a nasty trade-off, but one that must be faced implicitly or explicitly. My bias is to believe that recognizing the presence of the trade-off helps the system design problem, but then that is the underlying presumption in choosing to talk about the back-and-forth between theory and policy. I also suspect that some very high tax rates are appropriate.

The nastiness of this trade-off between revenue and disincentives makes the idea of targeting attractive. But the incentive approach recognizes that any attempt to draw lines between groups is itself a source of incentives (and also will be subject to both type I and type II errors, errors of overinclusion and overexclusion). For example, Aid to Families with Dependent Children (AFDC) affects family structure, but it permits a much better trade-off between income levels and incentives. Thus one needs to balance alternative packages of disincentives. Noting the effect of AFDC on family structure is the beginning, not the end, of analysis of such a program.

9.2 General Equilibrium

Another distinctive aspect of economists' reasoning is the use of general equilibrium. The fundamental welfare theorem tells us the circumstances under which idealized competitive markets give efficiency and how efficient outcomes can be achieved using competitive markets. This theorem plays a major role in organizing the thinking of economists on government interventions. The importance of the theorem comes not from its direct applicability but from its role in organizing the subject, shaping the discourse. As Frank Hahn (1973) has put it in his discussion of the optimal taxation literature, theory gives us a vocabulary, a grammar for talking about policy. Theory also shapes the way we make arguments and the ability of arguments to have legitimacy. We want to preserve the organizing role of the fundamental theorem, without becoming captive to the naive application of its results since real-world markets never work as well as those in the model.

A first point about general equilibrium is government budget balance in the appropriate (intertemporal) sense. This part of general equilibrium is visible to anyone worrying about the long-run budget imbalances that are so widespread today. So I want to focus on a second dimension of general equilibrium: risk allocation. This point is that risks do not disappear, they are allocated somewhere. The world is uncertain and that uncertainty must be borne somewhere. Some allocations spread some of the risk so widely that there is little risk aversion to handling this allocation. This is classic risk pooling by insurance companies and allocation of diversifiable risk through well-functioning capital markets. But not all risk falls in the category of diversifiable, and not all risk is allocated by these two mechanisms. So one question to ask of any system is where the risks are allocated and whether that is a good place to put them. In particular, different choices between defined benefit and defined contribution pension systems allocate risks differently among workers, future workers, capital owners, and future capital owners. One learns about the realization of important random variables at different times, and at any time different people are of different ages. The ability to bear risks depends on the age at which one learns about the outcomes one is subject to. This is particularly important for programs that affect the elderly. Thus the emphasis commonly put on the value of long lead times when cutting programs that affect the elderly has a firm basis in differential abilities to bear risks.

In thinking about patterns of risk bearing, it is important to recognize that we do not make allocation decisions once and for all. Individuals change their plans over time. Market possibilities change over time. And government actions change over time. Thus, in thinking about the pattern of risk allocation, one needs to ask how current decisions affect both future possibilities and the likelihood of alternative future decisions. This holds for mutual insurance companies as much as it does for government pension systems. Future legislation will generally take operational structures as given. So a public pension system that varies by industry will have political debates about different systems for different industries—coal miners versus academics, for example. In the United

States, the unitary social security system eliminates such debates (or shifts them elsewhere). Instead, we argue about the treatment of differently structured families and people born in different years, such as the "notch babies." And U.S. Social Security is small relative to retirement needs—commonly referred to as a floor or foundation for retirement income. Thus, differences in sensible retirement planning between, say, coal miners and academics, can be recognized in the different retirement systems developed in the different industries to supplement social security, subject to government regulation, not government decision.

9.3 Political Economy

This observation starts me on the subject of political economy. To organize our thinking, it is natural to divide the process of policy design into a strategic choice between approaches and a tactical choice of parameters within each strategic approach. Of course, these are not really separable since the best strategic choice depends on how the different tactical choices will be made. Where political economy has an important message is in recognizing that the strategic choices result in different politics that, in turn, will affect how the tactical choices will be made. For example, the government is equally capable of redistributions in defined benefit and defined contribution pension systems, but the common wisdom is that redistributions happen more often and to a greater degree with defined benefit than with defined contribution systems. This pattern seems as true of private pension systems as of public ones. When starting a company pension plan, it is customary to give past service credits when starting a defined benefit system, and it is very unusual to give similar initial wealth when starting a defined contribution system. (Indeed, a casual search has turned up no examples.) This is not due to any necessary logic in the differences between the two systems, but seems to be a fact of how people tend to see and use such systems, a point I return to.

Political economy is a very complicated subject, and I want to speak about one reason I find it so complicated. I continue with my earlier example. Defined benefit pensions are frequently highly redistributive, while defined contribution pensions are not. Even when they are not explicitly redistributive—for example, through a nonlinear benefit formula—they are redistributive from the nature of the determination of benefits. Such redistribution can readily be progressive or regressive. There is both opportunity and danger. It is common to refer to this difference as manipulation using details hidden from people; but I think that this is an incomplete description. The question is not whether one system is transparent while the other is not. The question is what is more visible or more salient with different systems. I suspect that differences in salience come from a similar underlying psychology as the sensitivity of opinion poll responses to the exact phrasing of questions. That is, there are well-known framing effects in polling, and I suspect similar effects in political discussion and political outcomes. Just as defined contribution systems make redistributions more visible, so defined benefit systems make patterns of outcomes more visible. The lack of visibility as to how much pensions will vary across people with defined contribution systems adds to their acceptability to the general public; that is, some of the consequences are hidden.

Thus, there is no easy way in which one appeals to "transparency" or "democratic outcomes" to judge among different patterns. When different agendas lead to different democratic outcomes, one can't appeal to the fact of democratic voting, given the agenda, especially when the questions are hard to analyze. There is a literature on the differences between representative democracy and direct democracy. And different outcomes come from different ways of organizing representative democracy, different allocations of power among voters, politicians, and civil servants. For example, Justice Stephen Breyer (1993) has written that the United States does a poor job of protecting people from health hazards because Congress is highly responsive to the public in this arena and the public is not good at making choices involving trade-offs between health and safety risks and money. Breyer calls for more of a role for civil servants, a call that reflects his respect for the performance of top-level civil servants in the United States. In effect, this is a call for less visibility. A similar view holds that liberal trade outcomes in the United States are helped by protecting Congress by use of fast-track rules and other processes that shift decision making toward the executive and away from the legislature. And the use of base-closing commissions serves a similar purpose. On the other hand, we all recognize that theft and patterns of transfers we disapprove of are also helped by decreased visibility.[1] The balance between the values of different kinds of increased and decreased visibility vary across countries, as does political culture. Policy recommendations need to reflect country differences.

---

1. For an excellent discussion of salience and politics, see Arnold (1990).

One example of the critical role of political predictions in policy recommendations is in the debate between those who favor having the U.S. Social Security Trust Fund invest directly in stocks and those who think that the investment would be done better with individual accounts. There are a number of political predictions that are cited on both sides of this debate (see, e.g., Diamond 1999a), but I want to consider just one—how well would the funds be invested.[2] All parties to the debate agree that investment decisions should not be made by Congress. The institutional design favored by proponents of such investment is meant to mimic the insulation from day-to-day politics in the designs of the Federal Reserve System and the Thrift Savings Board (which organizes investment options for the defined contribution pensions of federal civil servants). Indeed, proponents of individual accounts favor a similar structure when they include investment options that are presented by the government (rather than turning workers loose in the private market, as with IRA's). There is a debate of how well such insulation would protect investment, or more accurately, what differences there would be if such insulation were applied to individual accounts rather than Trust Fund investments.[3] But relevant to the issue here is the fact that both sides in this debate argue that civil servants, not elected

2. Another issue is whether government ownership would affect corporate behavior through the voting of shares or would affect other government behavior through particular concern about the values of stocks owned by the Trust Fund. For a general discussion, see Angelis (1998).

3. For analysis of how well U.S. state and local governments have done with such investments, see Munnell and Sundén (1999). I am not aware of a similar analysis of foreign experience in countries such as Denmark, Norway, and Sweden, which have had such investment for a while. More data points will be generated by the still-new experiences in Canada and Switzerland.

officials, should be making these decisions. That is, political economy needs to recognize both the endogenous choice of institutions and the likelihood that different institutions will function differently.

One needs to evaluate the outcomes of different agenda designs in terms of some set of criteria. And here analysts will often differ in the patterns of outcomes they think better. I fear that the best that analysts can do is to state the ethical principles underlying their choice of institutions in so far as they affect outcomes, and to state the assumptions about political evolution that underlie the forecasts. For political economy is still in its infancy, and our predictions will be full of errors. But then, that is an important part of the back-and-forth between theory and policy. Explicit analysis helps us recognize where theory is helping and where it is not helping and needs better development and/or better use.

Also important in grounding policy in theoretical models is the need to recognize differences across different models. For example, the simplest competitive models miss important aspects of the real working of markets. From the simplest models, one would argue that Chilean privatization of mandatory savings and annuity purchase/ phased withdrawal would have vastly lower administrative costs than the inefficient public system that was there before. But selling costs are not a part of the basic competitive model. And the reality is that the costs have not been all that different (Diamond 1994). Similarly, in the United States, the private life insurance industry has administrative costs per dollar of revenues that are roughly seven times those of the Social Security Administration. When moving from theory to its use, one needs to recognize both the insights of the theory and the extent of applicability of those insights; one needs to think about which lessons carry over from some particular model to some particular reality. Myopia, poor choices, limited understanding of risk/return trade-offs, the value of consumer sovereignty, bureaucratic errors, and misbehavior —these are all fair game for realistic discussions. But such discussion can be informed by theory. As Alfred Marshall (1948) put it:

it [is] necessary for man with his limited powers to go step by step; breaking up a complex question, studying one bit at a time, and at last combining his partial solutions into a more or less complete solution of the whole riddle.... The more the issue is thus narrowed, the more exactly can it be handled: but also the less closely does it correspond to real life. Each exact and firm handling of a narrow issue, however, helps towards treating broader issues, in which that narrow issue is contained, more exactly than would otherwise have been possible. With each step ... exact discussions can be made less abstract, realistic discussions can be made less inexact than was possible at an earlier stage. (p. 366)

Recapping, I would argue, first, that incentives really do matter. Pointing out implied poor incentives in a policy proposal is an important job of an analyst. But poor incentives are not a reason for inaction if the good effects of the program are important enough and there is no alternative route to the goals without comparably poor incentives. Disincentives need to be optimized, not set to zero. Second, risks are omnipresent and need to be recognized. Unsustainable programs are a particularly unattractive source of future risks. Third, programs will do better when they build on whatever political strengths may be present and hold down the potential for mischief from the political weaknesses that will also be present.

References

Allen, Franklin. 1982. "Optimal linear income taxation with general equilibrium effects on wages." *Journal of Public Economics* 17(2): 135–144.

Angelis, Theodore. 1998. "Investing public money in private markets: What are the right questions?" In *Framing the Social Security Debate, Values, Politics and Economics*, ed. R. Douglas Arnold, Michael J. Graetz, and Alicia H. Munnell, 287–315. Washington, DC: National Academy of Social Insurance, distributed by Brookings Institution Press.

Arnold, R. Douglas. 1990. *The Logic of Congressional Action*. New Haven: Yale University Press.

Arrow, Kenneth. 1963–1964. "The role of securities in the optimal allocation of risk-bearing." *Review of Economic Studies* 31(2): 91–96.

Atkinson, Anthony, and Joseph Stiglitz. 1976. "The design of tax structure: Direct versus indirect taxation." *Journal of Public Economics* 6(1): 55–75.

Auerbach, Alan, and Laurence Kotlikoff. 1987. *Dynamic Fiscal Policy*. Cambridge: Cambridge University Press.

Ben-Porath, Yoram. 1980. "The f-connection: Families, friends and firms, and the organization of exchange." *Population and Development Review* 6(1): 1–30.

Bernheim, B. Douglas. 1991. "How strong are bequest motives? Evidence based on esitmates of the demand for life insurance and annuities." *Journal of Political Economy* 99(5): 899–927.

Bernheim, B. Douglas, Lorenzo Forni, Jagadeesh Gokhale, and Laurence J. Kotlikoff. 2001. "The adequacy of life insurance: Evidence from the health and retirement survey." NBER Working Paper 7372.

Beveridge, W. H. 1943. *Social Insurance and Allied Services*. London: Cmd 6404, Her Majesty's Stationery Office.

Boadway, Robin, and Michael Keen. 1993. "Public goods, self selection and optimal income taxation." *International Economic Review* 34(3): 463–478.

Bohn, Henning. 1997. "Risk sharing in a stochastic overlapping generations economy." Unpublished, University of California at Santa Barbara.

Börsch-Supan, Axel. 2000a. "A model under siege: A case study of the german retirement insurance system." *The Economic Journal* 110(461): F24–45.

Börsch-Supan, Axel. 2000b. "Was lehrt uns die empirie in sachen renternrefor?" *Perspectiven der Wirtschaftspolitik* 1: 431–450.

Börsch-Supan, Axel, and Reinhold Schnabel. 1999. "Social security and retirement in germany." In *Social Security and Retirement Around the World*, ed. Jonathan Gruber and David Wise, 135–180. Chicago: University of Chicago Press.

Breyer, Friedrich. 2000. "Kapitaldeckungs versus umlageverfahren." *Perspectiven der Wirtschaftspolitik* 1, 383–405.

Breyer, Stephen. 1993. *Breaking the Vicious Circle: Toward Effective Risk Regulation*. Cambridge: Harvard University Press.

Brown, Jeffrey, and James Poterba. 2000. "Joint life annuities and the demand for annuities by married couples." *The Journal of Risk and Insurance* 67(4): 527–554.

Brugiavini, Agar. 1993. "Uncertainty resolution and the timing of annuity purchases." *Journal of Political Economy* 50(1): 31–62.

Burkhauser, Richard V., and Timothy Smeeding. 1994. "Social security reform: A budget neutral approach to reducing older women's disproportionate risk of poverty." Policy brief, Maxwell School, Syracuse University.

Carruth, Alan A. 1982. "On the role of the production and consumption assumptions for optimum taxation." *Journal of Public Economics* 17(2): 145–156.

Chatterjee, Satyajit. 1988. "Participation externality as a source of co-ordination failure in a competitive model." Unpublished, University of Iowa.

Choné, Philippe, and Guy Laroque. 2001. "Optimal incentives for labor force participation." Working Paper 2001-25, Institut national de la statistique et des etudes economiques, Centre de rescherche en economie et statistique.

Corlett, W. J., and D. C. Hague. 1953. "Complementarity and the excess burden of taxation." *Review of Economic Studies* 21(1): 21–30.

Crawford, Vincent, and David Lilien. 1981. "Social security and the retirement decision." *Quarterly Journal of Economics* 96(3): 505–529.

Davidoff, Thomas, Jeffrey Brown, and Peter Diamond. 2001. "Annuities and welfare." Unpublished, MIT.

Debreu, Gerard. 1951. "The coefficient of resource utilization." *Econometrica* 19(3): 273–292.

Debreu, Gerard. 1954. "A classical tax-subsidy problem." *Econometrica* 22(1): 14–22.

Diamond, Peter. 1967. "The role of a stock market in a general equilibrium model with technological uncertainty." *American Economic Review* 57: 759–776.

Diamond, Peter. 1973. "Taxation and public production in a growth setting." In *Models of Economic Growth*, ed. J. A. Mirlees and N. H. Stern, 215–240. London: MacMillan.

Diamond, Peter. 1977. "A framework for social security analysis." *Journal of Public Economics* 8(3): 275–298.

Diamond, Peter. 1980. "Income taxation with fixed hours of work." *Journal of Public Economics* 13(1): 101–110.

Diamond, Peter. 1994. "Privatization of social security: Lessons from Chile." *Revista de Analisis Economico* 9(4): 21–33.

Diamond, Peter. 1997. "Macroeconomic aspects of social security reform." In *Brookings Papers on Economic Activity* 2: 1–87.

Diamond, Peter. 1998. "Optimal income taxation: An example with a u-shaped pattern of optimal marginal tax rates." *American Economic Review* 88(1): 82–95.

Diamond, Peter, ed. 1999a. *Issues in Privatizing Social Security: Report of an Expert Panel of the National Academy of Social Insurance*. Cambridge: The MIT Press.

Diamond, Peter. 1999b. "Social security reform with a focus on Italy." *Revista Di Politica Economica* 89(12): 11–27.

Diamond, Peter. Forthcoming. *Social Security Reform, the 1999 Lindahl Lectures*. Oxford: Oxford University Press.

Diamond, Peter, and Botond Koszegi. 1999. "Quasi-hyperbolic discounting and retirement." MIT Working Paper. Forthcoming in *Journal of Public Economics*.

Diamond, Peter, and Daniel McFadden. 1974. "Some uses of the expenditure function in public economics." *Journal of Public Economics* 3(1): 3–21.

Diamond, Peter, and Eytan Sheshinski. 1995. "Economic aspects of optimal disability benefits." *Journal of Public Economics* 57(1): 1–23.

Diamond, Peter, and James Mirrlees. 1971. "Optimal taxation and public production 1 and 2." *American Economic Review* 61(1, 3): 8–27, 261–278.

Diamond, Peter, and James Mirrlees. 1978. "A model of social insurance with variable retirement." *Journal of Public Economics* 10(3): 295–336.

Diamond, Peter, and James Mirrlees. 1986. "Payroll-tax financed social insurance with variable retirement." *Scandinavian Journal of Economics* 88(1): 25–50.

Diamond, Peter, and James Mirrlees. 2000. "Adjusting one's standard of living: Two period models." In *Incentives, Organization and Public Economics, Papers in Honour of Sir James Mirrlees*, ed. P. J. Hammond and G. D. Myles, 107–122. Oxford: Oxford University Press.

Diamond, Peter, and James Mirrlees. Forthcoming. "Social insurance with variable retirement and private saving." *Journal of Public Economics*.

Dulitzky, Daniel. 1998. "Social security reforms, retirement plans, and saving under labor income uncertainty." MIT Ph.D. diss.

Feldstein, Martin. 1973. "On the optimal progressivity of the income tax." *Journal of Public Economics* 2(4): 32–36.

Feldstein, Martin. 1985. "The optimal level of social security benefits." *Quarterly Journal of Economics* 100(2): 300–320.

Foley, Duncan. 1970. "Economic equilibrium with costly marketing." *Journal of Economic Theory* 2(3): 276–291.

Gale, Douglas. 1990. "The efficient design of public debt." In *Public Debt Management: Theory and History*, ed. R. Dornbusch and M. Draghi, 14–47. Cambridge: Cambridge University Press.

Geanakoplos, John. 1990. "An introduction to general equilibrium with incomplete markets." *Journal of Mathematical Economics* 19(1): 1–38.

Gruber, Jonathan, and David Wise, ed. 1999. *Social Security and Retirement Around the World*. Chicago: University of Chicago Press.

Gruber, Jonathan, and Emmanuel Saez. 2000. "The elasticity of taxable income: Evidence and implications." NBER Working Paper 7521. Forthcoming, *Journal of Public Economics*.

Guesnerie, Roger, and Jesus Seade. 1982. "Nonlinear pricing in a finite economy." *Journal of Public Economics* 17(2): 145–156.

Hahn, Frank. 1971. "Equilibrium with transaction costs." *Econometrica* 39(2): 417–439.

Hahn, Frank. 1973. "On optimum taxation." *Journal of Economic Theory* 6(1), 96–106.

Harberger, Arnold. 1964. "The measurement of waste." *American Economic Review, Papers and Proceedings* 54(3): 58–76.

Hart, Oliver. 1975. "On the optimality of the equilibrium when the market structure is incomplete." *Journal of Economic Theory* 11(3): 418–443.

Holden, Karen, and Cathleen Zick. 1998. "Insuring against the consequences of widowhood in a reformed social security system." In *Framing the Social Security Debate, Values, Politics and Economics*, ed. R. Douglas Arnold, Michael J. Graetz, and Alicia H. Munnell, 157–170. Washington, DC: National Academy of Social Insurance, distributed by Brookings Institution Press.

Homburg, Stefan. 2000. "Ein schnellkurs in sachen rentenreform." *Perspektiven der Wirtschaftspolitik* 1: 379–382.

İmrohoroğlu, Ayşe, Selahattin İmrohoroğlu, and Douglas Joines. 2000. "Time inconsistent preferences and social security." Unpublished, University of Southern California.

Kahneman, Daniel, Paul Slovic, and Amos Tversky, eds. 1982. *Judgment Under Uncertainty: Heuristics and Biases* Cambridge: Cambridge University Press.

Kaplow, Louis. 1996. "The optimal supply of public goods and the distortionary cost of taxation." *National Tax Journal* 49(4): 513–533.

Kotlikoff, Laurence, and Avia Spivak. 1981. "The family as an incomplete annuities market." *Journal of Political Economy* 89(2): 372–391.

Kunreuther, Howard, and Paul Slovic. 1978. "Economics, psychology and protective behavior." *American Economic Review* 68(2): 64–69.

Laibson, David. 1997. "Golden eggs and hyperbolic discounting." *Quarterly Journal of Economic* 112(2): 443–478.

Magill, Michael, and Martine Quinzii. 1996. *Theory of Incomplete Markets*. Cambridge: MIT Press.

Marshall, Alfred. 1948. *Principles of Economics*, 8th ed. New York: Macmillan.

Mirrlees, James. 1971. "Exploration in the theory of optimal income taxation." *Review of Economic Studies* 38(114): 175–208.

Mirrlees. James. 1976. "Optimal tax theory: A synthesis." *Journal of Public Economics* 6(4): 327–358.

Mirrlees, James. 1986. "The theory of optimum taxation." In *Handbook of Mathematical Economics*, vol. III, ed. K. J. Arrow and M. D. Intriligator. Amsterdam: North-Holland.

Mitchell, Olivia, James Poterba, Jeffrey Brown, and Mark Warskawsky. 1999. "New evidence of the money's worth of individual annuities." *The American Economic Review* 89(5): 1299–1318.

Munnell, Alicia, and Annika Sundén. 1999. "Investment practices of state and local pension plans." In *The Next Challenge: Pensions in the Public Sector* ed. Olivia S. Mitchell and Edwin C. Hustead, 153–194. The Pension Research Council. Philadelphia: University of Pennsylvania Press.

Naito, H. 1999. "Re-examination of uniform commodity taxes under a nonlinear income tax system and its implications for production efficiency." *Journal of Public Economics* 71(2): 165–188.

Pagano, Marco. 1989. "Endogenous market thinness and stock price volatility." *Review of Economics Studies* 56(2): 269–287.

Quigley, John, and Eugene Smolenksy, ed. 1994. *Modern Public Finance.* Cambridge: Harvard University Press.

Rabin, Matthew. 2000. "Risk aversion and expected-utility theory: A calibration theorem." *Econometrica* 68(5): 1281–1292.

Rabin, Matthew, and Richard H. Thaler. 2001. "Anomolies: Risk aversion." *Journal of Economic Perspective* 15(1): 219–232.

Revesz, John. 1989. "The optimal taxation of labour income." *Public Finance* 44(3): 453–475.

Saez, Emmanuel. 1999. "A characterization of the income tax schedule minimizing deadweight burden." Unpublished, Harvard University.

Saez, Emmanuel. 2000a. "The desirability of commodity taxation under nonlinear income taxation and heterogeneous tastes." Working Paper 8029, NBER, December. Forthcoming in *Journal of Public Economics.*

Saez, Emmanuel. 2000b. "Optimal income transfer programs: Intensive versus extensive labor supply responses." NBER Working Paper 7708, May. Forthcoming, *Quarterly Journal of Economics.*

Saez, Emmanuel. 2000c. "The optimal treatment of tax expenditures." NBER Working Paper 8037, December.

Saez, Emmanuel. 2001. "Using elasticities to derive optimal income tax rates." *Review of Economic Studies* 68(1): 205–230.

Schmähl, Winfried. 2000. "Perspectiven der alterssicherungspolitik in deutschland—uber konzeptionen, vorschlage und einen angestrebten paradigmenweschel." *Perspektiven der Wirtschaftspolitik* 1: 407–430.

Schmidt-Hebbel, Klaus. 1999. "Latin America's pension revolution: A review of approaches and experience." Unpublished, Central Bank of Chile.

Schnabel, Reinhold. 1998. "Kapitalmartrenditen und die rendite der gesetzlichen rentenversicherung." Unpublished, Mannheim.

Schnabel, Reinhold. 1999. "Opting out of social security: Incentives and participation in the German public pension system." Discussion Paper 99-42 SFB 504, Mannheim.

Shafir, Eldar, Peter Diamond, and Amos Tversky. 1997. "Money illusion." *Quarterly Journal of Economics* 112(2): 341–374.

Sheshinski, Eytan. 1999. "Annuities and retirement." Department of Economics, The Hebrew University of Jerusalem.

Shiller, Robert. 1993. *Macro Markets: Creating Institutions for Managing Society's Largest Economic Risks, Clarendon Lectures*. Oxford: Oxford University Press.

Stiglitz, Joseph E. 1982. "Self-selection and pareto efficient taxation." *Journal of Public Economics* 17(2): 213–240.

Thum, Marcel, and Jakob von Weizsäcker. 2000. "Implizite einkommensteuer als messlatte fur die aktuellen reformvorshlage." *Perspektiven der Wirtschaftspolitik* 1: 453–468.

Tuomala, Matti. 1990. *Optimal Income Tax and Redistribution*. Oxford: Clarendon Press.

Valdés-Prieto, Salvador. 1998. "Risks in pensions and annuities: Efficient design." Technical Report, Social Protection Group, The World Bank.

Vickrey, William. 1947. *Agenda for Progressive Taxation*. New York: The Ronald Press Company.

Wilson, John D. 1982. "The optimal public employment policy." *Journal of Public Economics* 17(2): 241–258.

Wissenschaftlicher Beirat beim Bundesministerium. 1998. *Grundlegende Reform der gesetzlichen Rentenversicherung*. Bonn: Wissenschaftlicher Beirat beim Bundesministerium fur Wirtschaft.

Yaari, Menachem. 1965. "Uncertain lifetime, life insurance, and the theory of the consumer." *Review of Economic Studies* 32(2): 137–150.

Name Index

Subject Index